"As a pastor of a church where nearly nearly 70% of attendees are young adult and single, I know firsthand about the relational challenges many people face. Jumaine Jones provides practical knowledge and wise counsel to help anyone struggling to make sense of romantic disappointments."

 Mark Batterson, *Lead Pastor of National Community Church and New York Times bestselling author of The Circle Maker, In a Pit with a Lion on a Snowy Day, and Wild Goose Chase*

"What I love about Jumaine as well as his wife Dafnette's writing in this excellent work, is the fact that not only is the book both creative and engaging in its presentation, but it's also comprehensive in the information that it provides. You'll love the flow and feel of the book while being blessed by its rich content. I also love their transparency and the fact that they don't merely share lofty platitudes as if they've never struggled as singles or in marriage. But they open up their hearts and their lives and allow their personal stories of victories and defeats to build camaraderie and hope for us all."

 Keith Battle, *Lead Pastor, Zion Church in Largo, MD*

"Finding 'the one' remains one of the most important and challenging pursuits of our lives. Jumaine Jones shares a practical and insightful path towards becoming 'the one,' viewing romance with a healthy perspective, and avoiding a miserable marriage. The path towards romance combines both patience and proactivity—just as God intended."

 Dr. Eric Michael Bryant, *Pastor, Gateway Church in Austin, TX and author of Not Like Me: A Field Guide For Influencing A Diverse World*

"Jumaine Jones is truly one of the voices God is using to impact this generation. Jumaine Jones truly has a way of connecting with people of all ages and backgrounds. He ministers in a way that is fresh and creative, yet true to the Scriptures. His words are easy to understand, yet thought-provoking. He has a way of taking principles and making them come to life. I'm excited to see what God will continue to do through His servant."

Dr. Charles Gilmer, *President, The Impact Movement and author of A Call of Hope, A Call to Action*

LOST IN LOVE
NAVIGATING THE FIVE RELATIONSHIP TERRAINS

JUMAINE JONES

Lost In Love: Navigating the Five Relationship Terrains
Copyright 2013 by Jumaine Jones. All rights reserved.
ISBN 978-1-939676-06-1 (paperback).
Published by Dream Year.

All rights reserved. No part of this book may be reproduced or utilized in any form or by any means, electronic or mechanical, or by any information storage and retrieval system—except for brief quotations for the purpose of review, without written permission from the publisher.

Scripture taken from the NEW AMERICAN STANDARD BIBLE®, Copyright © 1960,1962,1963,1968,1971,1972,1973, 1975,1977,1995 by The Lockman Foundation. Used by permission.

Printed in the United States of America.

The names of people in this book have been changed to protect their privacy.

To My Beautiful Wife, Dafnette:
Thank you for your undying support and giving me the time and space to write my first book. I appreciate you opening your life to share in this book. Thanks for believing in me.

To My Family:
Thank you for your support throughout the years. Your love has helped shaped me into who I am.

To The Bridge:
I couldn't ask for a better church to pastor and be a part of.

CONTENTS

Chapter One: I'm Lost! 11
Chapter Two: The Mountain of Acceptance 27
Chapter Three: The Plateau of Comfort 47
Chapter Four: The Valley of One 63
Chapter Five: The Wilderness of Spectating 79
Chapter Six: The Land of Love 97
Chapter Seven: Our Story 115
Conclusion 133

CHAPTER ONE

I'M LOST!

I have a confession to make. I do not follow driving directions well. When someone tells me to turn right, I turn left. I think my wife grows weary of hearing me using the same joke a million times: "Oh, you meant the other left!" Not only am I directionally challenged when it comes to individual turns, I easily get lost when driving. After my wife and I moved into our first place, I got lost during one of my first trips home. I just kept circling around our neighborhood. I couldn't believe it! Who gets lost five minutes from his own home?

There's nothing like driving around and not knowing where you are. Thanks to phone apps and navigation systems, it's easy to discover our location, but this has not always been the case. Before personal navigation systems became readily accessible, someone wouldn't show up for the party because they couldn't find Jackson Avenue, or they found three Jackson Avenues in the same neighborhood. You can probably relate to taking a road trip and being set back for hours after taking the wrong exit off the highway. You had no idea you were lost on your way to Disney World until you saw a sign that read, "Welcome to Alabama!" It's frustrating not to know where you are.

The same is true of romance. We find ourselves making the wrong turns or driving around in relational circles. The journey began with the crush on the girl in first grade math. Then there was the cute cheerleader, the one you never had the courage to talk to until the 25th high school reunion. For others it started with the cute guy in seventh grade gym, then the handsome upperclassman who helped you find your locker.

The older we get, the more complex relationships become. In grade school, the only thing she had to do was check the "yes" box on the love letter. Ending the puppy love relationship in third grade may have caused you to shed a tear or two. But when we experience breakups as adults, the stakes are higher and the scars run deeper. We search for someone only to keep running into a dead end. We give our hearts only to be left brokenhearted and confused. We ask God to send the right person and meet someone we believe is the answer to our prayers, but the relationship fizzles out, leaving us confused and disillusioned. We feel lost.

THE RESPONSE OF THE LOST

Sometimes when driving I'll try to hide that I'm lost, talking nonchalantly with the other passengers as I secretly try to figure out where I need to go. But as much as we may try to hide it, eventually our responses make it obvious that we're lost. There are four ways we tend to respond.

1. *We feel hopeless and give up.* After a few hours of driving around in no-man's land, a sense of hopelessness can begin to set in. We start asking ourselves, "Is this really worth it?" We realize we've already missed half the show and think, "What's

the point?" We turn around and go back home.

The same is true with romance. After a few failed attempts, we begin to feel hopeless and we want to give up—on romance, and maybe on God. We may attend church services and be involved in church activities, but our faith has dried up. We stop praying because we stop believing. A few wrong turns leave us disillusioned.

2. We get frustrated and make bad decisions. Getting lost causes frustration and anger. Our blood pressure rises to a boiling point and we begin to make bad turns. We turn down streets because they "look right." Road rage festers and we become aggressive drivers who yell at other drivers. We curse, swear, run red lights, and make illegal U-turns. Similarly, we often allow failed relationships to make us turn to addictions and other destructive behaviors. We replace godliness with sin and cut off healthy friendships. We make U-turns by returning to old habits and lifestyle choices.

3. We pull over and ask the wrong person for directions. Asking someone for directions isn't always a bad idea. I've actually pulled over and asked for directions from people who have been extremely helpful. But this has not always been the case. I've asked people for directions who were unable to assist me. "Sorry, bud. I'm not from here." Others have tried to give me directions, but my unfamiliarity with the area rendered them useless. At other times, people have given me bad directions resulting in me remaining lost.

Not everyone is able to give good directions. Some people simply give bad relationship directions. Their advice is harmful and unwise. Others simply vent their own frustrations and you end up with a pity party of two people who are mad at God and the world. Some of our closest friends may even be ineffective, saying, "Beats me. I don't know what to tell you." There's no guarantee that asking for directions will help us find our way.

4. We keep driving and wing it. We drive around aimlessly, hoping we will eventually figure it out. We turn down streets, wrap around cul-de-sacs, and run into dead ends. Even though we may need to pull over and ask for directions, part of us says, "I'm fine. I'll figure it out." Likewise, we tend to drive around the neighborhood of romance cluelessly. We wing it, going from one relationship to the next. We say to ourselves, "I'm fine. I'll figure it out. I'll end up with the right person eventually." We wander around confused and distraught, collecting emotional baggage along the way.

A FEELING LIKE NO OTHER

Although we may feel lost in many areas of life—listening to a professor present information that goes over our heads, attending parties where we don't connect with anyone, moving to a new city and struggling to make friends—feeling lost in romance brings a burden unlike any other.

God created us as relational beings with a desire for intimacy. There's an inner longing to connect with our Creator and with people. No matter how hard we try, nothing else can fill the "God void." But there are also needs that can only be met by other people. We can commune with God on a regular basis and still feel lonely. And when we look for the human connection in a romance and don't find the love we desire, we feel lost.

IDOL OF ROMANCE

We often seek romance over friendship. We look to romantic

partners to fill the void that only God can fill and to provide the sense of community God intends for the body of Christ to provide. Because we idolize romance, relational disappointments rock us to the core. We can be left bitter and broken for years.

Mark Driscoll, the Lead Pastor of Mars Hill Church in Seattle, WA, puts it best. He says idolatry works like a religion. We find ourselves in a presumed hell. We feel our life is worthless without a romantic relationship. All our friends are dating and we feel left out. Our relatives and close friends are getting married one by one. We become angry, frustrated, and disillusioned and look to the god of romance to be our savior and take us to "heaven." We say, "Once I'm in a relationship, I will never be lonely again." "As soon as I become married, I will finally be happy and content." "Once I meet that special person, I'll be complete." The lyrics of pop songs describe lovers and romance as being like heaven. "Oh! You complete me, baby!" or "It's like heaven when you hold me in your arms!" or "I need you tonight! Hold me! Take control of me!"

You know romance has become an idol when it consumes you, becoming what you think and dream about the most. You can't imagine living the rest of your life without a romantic relationship. Romance drives you, dictating how you dress, the things you say, and where you spend your time. When romance becomes an idol, it sits on the throne of our hearts and becomes our lord.

The problem is no idol can bring redemption and eternal bliss. Created things aren't designed to bring us hope. The prophet Jeremiah speaks of idols being the work of skilled craftsmen, decorated with silver and gold. Idols can't speak or walk. We can shout to the god of romance, but it will not hear us. We can yell to it, but it will not deliver. Placing our hope in romance will always lead to disappointment because only Jesus Christ can bring ultimate satisfaction in our lives. As long as romance is your idol, you will always feel lost.

Many Christian singles have become polytheists; they claim to worship Jesus, but they also worship romance. They make sacrifices for someone that they would not make for Christ. They spend hundreds of dollars on gifts while giving almost nothing to their local church. They spend countless hours on the telephone and on dates, but won't use their gifts, talents, and time in serving others.

Idolizing romance eventually leads us to idolizing people. Whenever a person enters our life, they immediately become another god. Our world becomes consumed with them. We begin to hold this person to unrealistic expectations, wanting them to serve us and give us the kind of attention only God can give.

This kind of relationship usually ends in frustration and bitter disappointment. We must be determined to serve one God. Not a woman and God. Not a man and God. Not marriage and God. But God and God alone.

Punch a few holes in the bottom of a plastic cup, then try to fill it with water. The cup may be able to hold the water for a short time, but soon all the water will drip out. This is what idols do in our lives—they may provide temporary satisfaction, but they won't bring us ultimate fulfillment.

Some of the things we idolize are otherwise good things! Romance is a good thing—even a beautiful thing! A romantic relationship can make you smile and it may bring you a sense of happiness. But when romance becomes an idol it can be destructive. Ironically, when given the room in our life that God deserves, romance can leave us lonely and depressed and can destroy our self-esteem.

UNSURE OF THE DESTINATION

Have you ever asked someone where he's going and he can't give you a concrete answer? "Well, I think I'm supposed to be going to Franklin Avenue or Garden Square. Not quite sure. I'm sure it's around here somewhere. I think it's a white or blue building."

The more sure you are of your destination, the greater your chance of finding it. But many people aren't quite sure what they should be looking for in a future mate. They tend to be driven by their feelings rather than a set of virtues. And if you are unsure of your destination, you probably won't know you've arrived when you get there. Many singles have met the "right person," but still insist on searching for something else. Some get married, then drift towards infidelity. They continue searching.

One evening, my wife and I were on our way to the home of a couple in our small group. Without paying attention to the house number, we walked up to the house and almost knocked on the door. Suddenly we realized we were at the wrong house! The house looked exactly like the one we'd visited before, but we saw unfamiliar faces through the window and noticed the front of the house was dimly lit.

There are some individuals who will look like the type of person you want to be with. There are people who will make you feel the way you think the right person should make you feel. There may also be people who appear "God-sent." Unfortunately, you will discover that you, too, pulled up to the wrong address. Just because it feels right doesn't meant it is, and you won't know unless you first know what you're really looking for.

THE FIRST STEP

It may seem like a cliché, but it's true: the first step in finding your way is admitting that you're lost. Many drivers are afraid to admit they're not where they want to be. They say things like, "Looks like I made a minor detour somewhere." No, you didn't take a minor detour. You're lost! Many wives would fall in love with their husbands all over again if they simply admitted they were lost.

Isaiah 53:6 says, "All of us like sheep have gone astray, each of us has turned to his own way." Sheep tend to get distracted. Admit it to yourself—you're a sheep! We all have a proclivity to drift off the path God intended for us to follow. This is why sheep need a shepherd. Admitting you're lost is admitting that you're broken and you need a Shepherd. Admitting you're lost could be the turning point in your life if it forces you to ask, "Where am I?" Once we identify our current location, we can determine what we need to do to reach our destination.

DISCOVERING A MAP

When I was single and desiring a wife, I repeatedly ended up in situations not knowing where I stood. There were times I felt rejected. There were times when I did the rejecting. There were times I admired young ladies from afar and then decided to pump the breaks. On other occasions, I responded like a champ. I prayed, depended on God, and left the outcome to Him. Other times I bickered and complained. Sometimes, it felt like I just wasted my time.

One day, during my devotional time with God, I read Deuteronomy 2. This passage of scripture gives an account of the Israelites as they begin their journey towards Canaan and records a few stops the Israelites made on their way to the Promised Land. Along their journey, the Israelites encountered other nations and various groups of people. I observed the way God told them to relate to these people and the different terrains they traveled. Suddenly, something struck me! I noticed several relationship stages!

I was dumbfounded, but as I did more research and dug a bit deeper, the relationship terrains became clearer to me. The stages weren't linear. They were just different phases of life people tended to find themselves in before they finally met the right person who became their spouse.

As I examined these stages, I realized I had experienced them. As a matter of fact, I had been through some of the stages more than once. Some I even experienced at the same time! Not only that, but I knew other people who were experiencing the same thing.

As God began to unfold these insights, I held a pastoral position and had recently started a singles event at the church. I shared my thoughts about the stages at our monthly singles event. Exactly one week after sharing that message, I met my future wife for the first time. I kid you not! This means, if you apply the principles presented in this book, you will meet your future spouse in exactly seven days! (Just kidding.)

Anyway, I know what you're probably thinking: "Where's the map? I need it now! I'm lost! Besides, I only have seven days!" Not so fast. As we all know, there's some prep work that has to be done before embarking on any journey. Although you're eager to hit the pavement, there are three things we need in order to survive on this journey.

WE NEED BREAD

Food is critical for any journey. Ask anyone who has embarked on a hiking trip without food and they will tell you how important it is to come prepared. Today we have the convenience of stopping at a restaurant or grocery. Even gas stations now have convenient stores. Some even have fast food or full-fledged restaurants! They've realized, "Hey! If people are going on a journey, they are going to need food!"

You don't know how long your romantic journey will be. Some people get married at 20, others at 30, 40 or older. You may not be able to control the length of the journey, but you can control your food along the way.

Jesus said in John 6:35, "I am the bread of life." We eat when we partake of God's divine Word. His Word is nourishment to our soul.

When I was a child, our family owned a dog named Benji. Benji was a beautiful collie. We loved feeding him, and enjoyed watching him eat. I especially liked it when Benji licked around his bowl. It gave me a sense of pride to know that I fed him. But sometimes Benji would choose not to eat. He would sniff his food, then go back to whatever he was doing at the time. We realized we couldn't force Benji to eat. He had a choice.

Many Christians are like Benji—they choose not to eat. God has provided spiritual delicacies for us to dine on in the pages of His Word. Jesus is the Master Chef, yet we often reject His cooking. As a result, we become malnourished and approach relationships lacking the wisdom of God. It's not about trying to grab the Bible and find a verse for when we feel we've fallen in love. It's about constantly feeding on His Word.

Here are some reasons why we choose not to eat.

1. We tend to snack on junk food. We fill ourselves with junk food. Sexual immorality flashes on the television screen. Humanistic ideologies blast over the radio waves overlaid with great rhythms. Conversations with our friends are filled with inappropriate jokes. One bite leads to another, and eventually we don't have enough room left for the real food of God's truth and grace.

I love sweets, but they can ruin my appetite for dinner. Our flesh seems to crave anything that is sweet and fattening. The sweet treats of popular culture taste good in the moment but they spoil our appetite for God's Word and don't feed us for the long haul.

Sometimes we have to be like a child who can't play video games until he finishes his vegetables. We have to force ourselves to eat, even when we don't feel hungry. The more we dine on God's Word, the more we will grow to love it. We will increase in wisdom and discernment and we will be more prepared for the journey that lies ahead.

2. We are afraid to try something new. I once attended an event with friends where Caribbean food was being served. One of my friends decided to play it safe, staying away from the Caribbean cuisine and selecting more familiar choices. We said, "How could you be at a Caribbean event and not eat Caribbean food?" She said, "No offense. I'm just sticking with what I know."

Too often, we stick with what we know—the wisdom of the world. God's Word intimidates us or causes us to feel extremely uncomfortable. But the tension is good. God wants to shake up our paradigm and change our way of thinking. The internal change will prepare you for where He is taking you externally. Remember, God's ways are not our ways. His thoughts are not our thoughts.

3. We choose to skip lunch. Many of us can relate to working through our lunch hour. If you're like me, you rarely take lunch breaks. Even though we are hungry, we choose to skip a meal to work or to save time.

We often skip Scriptural meals for other things that seem urgent. Our children cry out, "Feed me!" Our early morning commute cries out, "Don't forget me! I need you to get to work on time." Errands say, "Where are you? You were supposed to take care of me last week! Am I not important to you?" Our friends insist, "You must attend this concert!" Our course work threatens, "If you don't complete me, I will make you fail." As a result, we say, "God, I love You, but I'll get back with You later. I promise. I'll eat…later."

Other times, we grab just a morsel, but not enough to fully feed us. We go to the snack machine of scripture and grab a few little verses, but we never fill our plate. We may hear an insightful sermon and say, "How did he come up with that? Wow! I can't believe that's in the Bible!" The teacher didn't do anything magical—he carved out time in his schedule to partake of hearty Scriptural meals. You didn't. That's all.

I once saw a pastor wearing a t-shirt that said, "Hungry? Feed yourself." Don't place your spiritual diet in the hands of someone else. Don't depend on a teacher, pastor, or leader to be your only source of spiritual nourishment. Feed yourself. Some of life's greatest lessons are found when we search the scriptures for ourselves.

4. We suffer spiritual bulimia. Some people lack spiritual nutrition, but it's not because they fail to eat. They just throw it up as soon as it's swallowed. They don't allow the food to digest and make its way throughout their digestive system. We "throw up" God's Word when we fail to listen to it or apply it. We get excited over new, scriptural insights and mentally stimulating ideas. We may even love how the Word of God makes us feel. But we dread applying God's Word to our lives. In the parable of the sower, Jesus says some seeds fall on stony ground, failing to take root and produce fruit. It's not enough to be hearers of the Word—we must also be doers of the Word.

WE NEED WATER

Water quenches our thirst and prevents us from dehydrating. In John 4, a Samaritan woman came to Jacob's Well for water and encountered Jesus, who said He could grant her Living Water so she'd never be thirsty again. He said in John 4:14, "The water that I will give him will become in him a well of water springing up to eternal life."

Jesus offered a Spirit-filled life. Realizing our need for water is like recognizing our need for the Holy Spirit. A Spirit-filled life is a life of worship and yielding to God's will. It's a life filled with the presence of God and marked by the desire to be right with God. In Psalm 51, David pleaded to the Lord, saying, "Create in me a clean heart, O God, and renew a steadfast spirit within me." When we spend time in God's Word, we become filled with His Spirit and the fruit of God's Spirit begins to radiate throughout our lives.

Psalm 1 says the person who delights in God's instructions will be like a tree planted by the rivers of water that brings fruit in its season. This tree is constantly nourished and life flows through it. The tree may not bear fruit right away. In the fall or winter it may appear fruitless. It may even look like a lifeless accumulation of dead branches. But when spring and summer arrive, the fruit is abundant. Spending time in God's presence may not immediately bring about discernable results. But over time, God begins to purge, nourish and enrich you. Your behavior, speech, outlook, paradigm, thought patterns, and perspective all begin to change. You develop a Spirit-filled life.

WE NEED A MAP

A map is vital when traveling to an unknown territory. A map gives us a bird's eye view of our journey and helps us get from where we are to where we need to be.

The relationship journey can be difficult to navigate. Not only do we feel lost, we're also unsure of what to do next. We may go through the motions of a relationship but be unsure of what practical steps to take. We may be in an evolving relationship, but unsure of where we really stand with the other person. We may find ourselves stuck in a dead-end relationship. We may find ourselves looking forward to marrying someone only for the relationship to end. We may know we should pray, read scripture, and seek counsel. Yet, there's an undeniable fog that often remains.

What if we had a relational map? What if we had a way of discovering exactly where we are? By knowing where we are, we can navigate our way back to God's path. Drivers need a road map. Hikers need a trail map. Sailors need a nautical map. Those who desire to be in a romantic relationship need a relationship map. The following pages of this book will provide you with a relational map so you can get where God wants you to be. It's time to stop being lost in love!

THE RELATIONAL MAP

The purpose of the relational map is to help us identify where we are so we know what to do to get where God wants us to be. The map contains five relationship terrains. At some point, everyone find themselves in one of these terrains. We can even find ourselves going through more than one simultaneously. The relational map doesn't function like a subway map for people who plan to go from stop to stop. It is simply to help us make sense of where we are. Even though we desire to hear from God, we are still subject to our own humanity. Even the person with the right intentions, who seeks to wait on God's timing, can find himself in unfortunate relational circumstances.

So throughout this book, we will cover five relationship terrains:

- The Mountain of Acceptance: The place where you must accept that something good is not intended for you.
- The Plateau of Comfort: The place where you settle for a relationship because it's comfortable.
- The Valley of One: The place where God desires to have our undistracted devotion to Him.
- The Wilderness of Spectating: The place where you watch others who have a relationship you want.
- The Land of Love: The place where you enlist in a lifelong commitment to fight for your marriage.

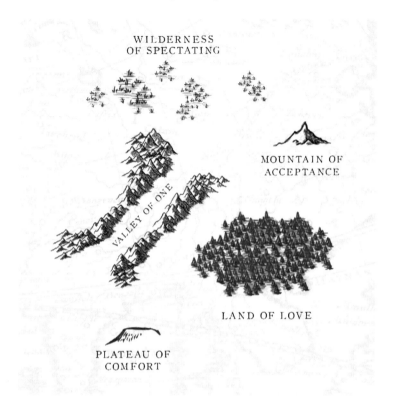

LANDMARKS

- The first step to getting on the proper course is admitting I'm lost.
- Idolizing romance causes me to feel lost.
- In order to survive the relational journey, I need bread, water, and a relational map.
- A relational map helps us to identify where we are, so we know what we need to do to get where God wants us to be.

CHAPTER TWO

THE MOUNTAIN OF ACCEPTANCE

Then we turned and set out for the wilderness by the way to the Red Sea, as the Lord spoke to me, and circled Mount Seir for many days. And the Lord spoke to me, saying, "You have circled this mountain long enough. Now turn north, and command the people, saying, 'You will pass through the territory of your brothers the sons of Esau who live in Seir; and they will be afraid of you. So be very careful; do not provoke them, for I will not give you any of their land, even as little as a footstep because I have given Mount Seir to Esau as a possession. You shall buy food from them with money so that you may eat, and you shall also purchase water from them with money so that you may drink. For the Lord your God has blessed you in all that you have done; He has known your wanderings through this great wilderness. These forty years the Lord your God has been with you; you have not lacked a thing (Deuteronomy 2:1-7).'"

The first place the Israelites arrived was Seir. Seir is described as a hill country; a mountain; an elevated place. It was a place where you could stand on top and get a tremendous view across the skies as well as into the valleys below.

God told Moses the Israelites would have to pass through this region. They anticipated encountering the descendants of Esau, the Edomites. Because their ancestor Jacob had deceived his father and dishonestly received the blessings that should have gone to his brother Esau, there was tension between the two groups.

Naturally, the sons of Esau were afraid of the Israelites wandering through their territory. They probably assumed the Israelites were coming to attack. Therefore, Moses warned the people, "Be careful and don't provoke them." God went on to make something very clear to the Israelites, telling them He would not be giving them any of the Edomites' land. They were not going there to settle, and He wasn't calling them to divide and conquer. Instead, this was just a land they would pass through and they would simply exchange their money for the Edomites' goods. That was the purpose of the relationship.

GOOD THING

As you travel this journey of romance, you may find yourself on The Mountain of Acceptance. The Mountain of Acceptance is where you must accept that a particular good thing is not intended for you. Three things mark The Mountain of Acceptance:

1. Elevated Terrain. You encounter good people there. As a matter of fact, you may even encounter amazing people: a beautiful woman or a respectful man, maybe even someone who will make you laugh and cry tears of joy. You will meet someone with whom you share great chemistry. You will have a relationship with a person who seems second-to-none. It may be a co-worker or a person at a church with whom you enjoy great fellowship. This may be a person you can talk to for hours, even as the janitor begins sweeping the church floors or the security guards have begun closing the doors. Being in this person's presence feels like a mountain top experience. It may even be the best romantic relationship you've ever experienced. You begin to believe this is the person God has for you. Your joy and expectancy are noticeably heightened on The Mountain of Acceptance.

2. *Exchange.* There is something you share with a person that makes the relationship special. Maybe you exchange looks. Maybe you exchange kind words. Maybe you give one another a piece of your hearts. Maybe you share the gospel of Christ and they give their heart to God. Consider this, when you make recurring exchanges with an organization or a person, you begin to feel connected. People who exchange currency for clothing at the same department store for years feel a sense of relationship. It's not just a store, it's your store. You will shop at that store even if the items you typically purchase are less expensive elsewhere. Similarly, the more you share with someone, the more your heart becomes connected. The greater the exchange, the greater the bond—and it's possible to feel like the commitment level of relationship is deeper than it really is.

3. *Acceptance.* This is the most difficult aspect of this terrain. Despite elevated emotions and favorable exchanges, there comes a point when you have to accept this is not where God wants you. You discover this relationship is not a place for you to stick the flag of a life-long romance.

Various factors can lead to this discovery. Maybe you feel deeply in love with the person, but their feelings for you remain shallow. Maybe the other person is interested in you, but you're not interested in them. For some, God may reveal red flags that are too numerous to ignore. No matter what the specifics, the bottom line is you realize you cannot move forward with the relationship and you must accept it. Keith Battle, the pastor of Zion Church in Maryland, always says, "Maturity accepts what God allows." At this level of terrain, you must be willing to embrace God's sovereignty and remember God is ultimately in control.

DOWNHILL

At some point, you have to come off the mountain, and the only way to leave The Mountain of Acceptance is to walk downhill. When it comes to relationships, descending the mountain can be as difficult as the climb up. Rarely have I met a person who doesn't experience an unwelcome emotional weight during their descent. The journey down may bring prolonged sorrow and regret. The level of conversations and quantity of time spent with the other person changes, and you may even have to sit back and watch them move on to another relationship. Like it or not, you have to accept the message God declared to the Israelites: "I have saved this land for Esau." This "land" is not meant for you.

There are several difficulties you may have to face on your way down the hill as you accept this reality.

1. Saying Goodbye to the "Perfect" Person. One of the most difficult relationship challenges we can face is not loving a difficult person. Rather, it's being attracted to the perfect person who is off-limits to us. It's the young lady with whom you have chemistry, great conversation, and fun times, or the kind man who listens to you and treats you with respect. This person appears to be the man or woman of your dreams. They seem to be an answer to prayer!

When we encounter these individuals, we become lovesick

and imagine our future with them. So when you discover this relationship will go no further than a friendship, it is heartbreaking. It shatters our dreams to be on the receiving end of comments like, "I think you're a great person, but…" "You're awesome, beautiful, handsome, godly, fun to be with, but…" "I would still like for us to be friends."

Deep inside you wish you could be honest and say, "I don't want your friendship! I have enough friends! I want your love!" You decide to go along with the friendship while praying for a ray of hope. You use "friendship" as a means to keep your foot in the door while allowing your heart to remain involved. Months or even years later, you decide to revisit the possibility of a deeper relationship. Guess what? You get the same response as you did two years ago: "I think you're a great, godly, and wonderful person, but…" You finally realize this is a closed door. This is not the person God has for you. And the longer you stay on the mountain, the more difficult it is to leave.

2. *Saying "I'm not interested."* Sometimes, the problem is not the other person. It's you. You meet someone amazing, but you don't love the person like he or she loves you. We sometimes have difficulty accepting these feelings because we are afraid of being alone. We would rather lead a person on and take advantage of the attention he gives us than be honest about our true feelings.

But every time we make an emotional deposit into someone's life, his or her love bank account grows. We create a desire we don't intend to fulfill. It's a build-up for a let-down. If for some reason you already know a relationship will not work, have the courage to let the person go. You are simply delaying the inevitable and you may be hindering them from moving forward and meeting the person God may have for them.

3. *Trying to Figure Out God.* Sometimes, it's difficult to make sense of the hand of God that we clearly saw in the relationship. We can see how God allowed us to meet the person, but we draw the wrong conclusions as to why God brought the person into our lives. We can know the "what," but not the "why." God may have brought a person into your life simply to be a light or source of spiritual encouragement. Maybe God intended the person to provide the assistance you needed for a particular task. Sometimes God brings people in our lives to test us or reveal important truths about ourselves. He may allow our paths to cross with someone we are attracted to in hopes that we would not yield to the temptation to compromise. He may use people to test our faith, trust, and dependence on Him. Maybe God just wanted to show us that godly men and women with pure motives exist!

We often assume the person was brought into our lives for romantic purposes, but we draw these conclusions without finding out God's will on the matter. Once God's purpose has been accomplished, He brings that chapter of our lives to a close. The quicker you can get on God's page, the sooner you can move on, and the sooner you can move on, the healthier you will be emotionally.

We must caution against drawing premature conclusions. We may connect with someone we're attracted to and see it as a sign from God. Think about it! We connect with people who we are not attracted to, but never see that connection as a sign from God. Is the driving force really a divine connection or our own attraction? Can it truly be a divine connection if a relationship requires mutual consent, yet you're the only one who desires the relationship?

Jeremiah 17:9 says the heart is deceitful above all things and desperately wicked. All we like sheep have gone astray. For this reason, like the psalmist in Psalm 23:1 we must say, "The Lord is my Shepherd." Sheep have a tendency of wondering off the path. The job of the shepherd is to guide the sheep. As the sheep drifts, the shepherd uses his rod to redirect it and get it back on track. Like sheep, we have a tendency to drift to the left and right. Even the most spiritual person with the best intentions can begin veering off the path. The Shepherd uses the staff of His Word, prayer, discernment, and circumstances to steer us back to a place of focus. When relationships don't pan out the way we expect, we have to say with confidence, "The Lord is my Shepherd." We may not like or agree with what He is doing, but He's sovereign. You must say, "While on the mountain, I will accept Your will."

As a single man, there were times I had to accept God's sovereignty. For some reason, He didn't allow certain relationships to progress. Sometimes, I was interested in a young lady, but she did not share my interest. On other occasions, a young lady was interested, but I was not. Each scenario brought some level of disappointment. Even though I am married to a godly, beautiful woman now, those situations were difficult at the moment. It was never pleasant to see fun exchanges and stimulating conversations come to an end. But if I was going to follow my Shepherd, I had to grab my belongings and move on.

MOVING ON

Leaving The Mountain of Acceptance may be difficult or complex. Sometimes it requires more than having a difficult conversation. You may live with the person and have to move out. Conflict may arise that requires involving police authorities or legal action. You may have to have several lengthy conversations so the other person truly understands. You may find yourself having to explain your decision to all your friends who now view you as the bad guy. You may have to deal with the cold shoulder you receive from your ex's friends and family members. Some people linger in fruitless relationships because they don't want to deal with the inevitable challenges associated with descending the mountain of acceptance. You may say, "Oh, well! Why not? I'll just give it another shot." The other person becomes excited that you are willing to give the relationship "another chance." But in time you can't ignore the little, tiny nudging inside telling you to move on. In time, you tire of the view from atop The Mountain of Acceptance. Like the children of Israel, you've overstayed your welcome. The quicker you can move on from a dating or courtship relationship that God doesn't intend to last, the better. Prolonging your departure only make things worse.

Sometimes we leave the mountain physically, but remain there mentally. The relationship is over, but mentally we are still consumed with fantasies of what might be. Years later we still refer to her as our girlfriend. We can even be married and still have feelings for an ex-girlfriend or boyfriend. When reminiscing we inadvertently tell others that he's our boyfriend. We speak of the past relationship using the present tense. Out of the abundance of the heart, the mouth speaks—evidently, we have not let go.

The Mountain of Acceptance is where you must accept God's will. In fact, you must embrace it! We wrestle and argue with God. We say, "How do I know it's God's will for the relationship to end? What if the other person is ignoring God's will for us to be together?"

Accepting God's will requires accepting what He allows to happen. The situation did not happen without going through God's desk of approval. It is not our job to find out whether or not a person is out of God's will for not wanting to love us. Our job is to align our will with His. In the Garden of Gethsemane, Jesus prayed to the Father, "Not my will, but thine be done." When teaching His disciples to pray, Jesus said, "Thy kingdom come, thy will be done on earth as it is in heaven."

In other words, our prayer needs to be "God, align my will on earth to your will in heaven. Align my agenda to your agenda. God, may I abandon building my romantic kingdom for your kingdom. May I not be consumed with this person, but be consumed with You. God, I take my heart from this person and I give it to you. May I knock down the idol that I have constructed in my mind and replace it with worship of the true and living God. May my thoughts of this person be exchanged for thoughts of You. May conversations in which I always bring up her name be exchanged for conversations in which Your name is brought to the forefront."

HOPE ASSURED

Here is the hope God gave the Israelites: "For the Lord your God has blessed you in all that you have done; He has known your wanderings through this great wilderness. These forty years the Lord your God has been with you; you have not lacked a thing" (Deuteronomy 2:7).

This statement assured Israel of two things:

1. They were assured of God's provision. Leaving the mountain empty-handed can cause one to question God. So God reminded the Israelites that for all the years they traveled through the great wilderness, He provided for them. They may not have had the luxuries and possessions they wanted, but they had everything they needed. God reminded them, "I fed you manna every day. When you were thirsty, I gave you water." And God did the most amazing thing—He caused their shoes to never wear out! Can you imagine having one pair of shoes that last for your entire life? God reminded them they had never lacked anything, and since He had provided for them in the past, He would provide for them in the future.

Let's be honest. When a relationship doesn't swing in our direction, we often question God's ability to provide. Watching a person walk out the door can shatter our faith. When we lose confidence in God's ability to provide, we seek to provide for ourselves. We feel we can do a better job than God. However, instead of taking matters into our own hands, we should take some time and reflect on ways God provided in the past. He has provided everything you needed up to this point. He even throws in extras we don't need! If God has provided our rent, mortgage, food, shelter, education, and employment, isn't He able to provide us a spouse? He can provide a mate for you, if that's His will for you. Reflecting on God's faithfulness in the past gives us hope for the future.

Just because God did not grant you someone on The Mountain of Acceptance does not negate God's ability. He remains Yahweh Yireh—the Lord who Provides. We can't base God's faithfulness or goodness on a relationship woe. We can't assume God will not provide because He hasn't worked on our timetable and yielded Himself to our will.

2. *They were assured of God's presence.* God told them that for

forty years, He had been with them. You must always remember that even though you may not have what you want, you have God's presence. God assures us He will never leave or forsake us. His presence is there to comfort and strengthen us.

When I look back at past situations, I now understand why God didn't allow them to work out. During my early adulthood, I had no idea where God would have me now. I had hopes, dreams and visions of what my future may be, yet I was not privy to the future details of my life and how God's plan for me would ultimately unfold. In hindsight, I realize that God knew exactly what I needed. He knew that it would take a certain type of woman to complement me and the calling on my life. He also knew the type of husband my wife needed to complement her and His will for her life.

In 1 Corinthians 13:12, the apostle Paul said, "For now we see in a mirror dimly, but then face to face." When it comes to the future, our knowledge and vision is partial at best. We are unable to sit outside of eternity and see all of life. We imagine that the ability to see the future would make our lives easier. After all, we could prepare if we knew what the future held.

Nevertheless, God has chosen for the just to live by faith. Faith sometimes requires wandering in the dark not knowing where we will end up. We have to watch people walk out of our lives without proper closure. We have to watch people hurt us and never fully understand the reason. When we look back years from now, things will make more sense. All we can do is embrace God's will for today. Jesus says in Matthew 6:34, "So do not worry about tomorrow; for tomorrow will care for itself. Each day has enough trouble of its own."

As the Israelites journeyed towards the Promised Land, according to Exodus 13:21, a cloud guided them by day and pillar of fire by night. When the cloud lifted up, it was a signal for the Israelites to move. The quicker you can move with the cloud, the quicker you can move on with your life. The quicker you can accept God's will, the quicker you can move on with the affairs of your life and His kingdom.

Heartbreak on The Mountain of Acceptance can bring a sense of loneliness. We can begin to feel like we're all alone. Even though friends may surround us, not having a companion can make us feel like we are being marginalized. We can begin to feel like no one quite understands us or we are being ignored.

Rest assured that God is sympathetic to your plight. Moses told Israel in Deuteronomy 2:7, "He has known your wanderings." God is aware of all the disappointments and loneliness we feel. His ear is not turned and He's not far off. He waits for us to commune with Him; we can take all of our burdens and lay them at the feet of the cross. He is our High Priest and can sympathize with our weaknesses. He stands as a Healer and Comforter. He is a Shield and Strong Tower. He's a shelter in a time of storm. He loves us and has provided a safe place where we can be honest and transparent about how we really feel.

Psalm 62:8 says, "Trust in Him at all times, O people; Pour out your heart before Him; God is a refuge for us." There's often a correlation between trust and transparency. The more we trust someone, the more open and honest we are. The more we trust God, the more willing we are to pour out our hearts before Him. Trusting God begins by realizing He is with us and He pays attention. As we run to His presence, we will find comfort, strength, and abundant grace. He showers us with loving-kindness. Even when we make mistakes and jump out in haste, He gracefully forgives and restores us. The greatest thing we can do is remember God is with us. Having a sense of His presence assures us we are safe. It reminds us that we aren't alone and He will work all things together for our good.

WATCH OUT FOR THORNS

We must be mindful of thorns and thistles on mountainous terrain. Failing to accept what God allows increases the likelihood of falling into thorny patches. While the pain we feel is already great, thorns leave more profound scars. When we fail to let relationships go, we may cause others to fall into the patch alongside us. When we move forward in acceptance, we remove distractions and avoid four hazardous thorns.

1. The Thorn of Possession. Accepting God's will prevents us from becoming possessive. Sometimes, we can sense when the tide changes in a relationship. We may notice the other person has doubts so we switch into life preserver mode and try to save the relationship. We make more phone calls. We begin to keep a tighter watch on the person we adore. We become jealous of any person of the opposite sex who shares her life. Even when the other person has made it clear that he or she does not want to move forward in the relationship, we hold on to the slightest ray of hope. As time passes, and the other person pursues relationships with others, we become bitter. In our minds, the person can be in no other relationship except with us.

2. The Thorn of Deception. When we prefer to have our way rather than accept God's will, we can resort to deception. We first deceive ourselves into thinking we can devise plans that will lead to the outcome we desire. We sow discord to cause division between two people in hopes of splitting them up. We may not think of ourselves as deceptive, but when we become desperate, even God's will seems like a bad idea. We may even resort to manipulative measures to keep someone in a relationship.

Remember, Jeremiah 17:9 says the heart is deceitful and sick. Many people will tell you to follow your heart but following your heart is placing yourself on a track that leads to disaster. I have seen otherwise godly Christ-followers do the most deceitful things when they become consumed with satisfying their desires. Take King Saul, for example. He could not accept that God had chosen David to replace him as king. His grave displeasure led to anger, jealousy and eventually attempts to kill David. Can you imagine that? The king you looked up to being convicted for attempted murder? Because God's power is greater than ours, we're reduced to deceptive schemes if we seek to override His will.

3. The Thorn of Bitterness. Accepting God's will prevents bitterness from festering. Far too often, we leave romantic relationships with bitterness in our hearts. We agree to go our separate ways, but we aren't fully convinced that the relationship should end. We agree to be friends, but become bitter that the person we loved can readily move on.

Hebrews 12:15 and Deuteronomy 29:18 refer to bitterness as a root. The root of bitterness entangles itself around your heart and other relationships. The longer bitterness resides in your heart, the deeper the roots grow. The only way to prevent bitterness from overtaking the heart is by uprooting it.

Uprooting bitterness early is comparable to pulling up weeds. If we allow weeds to grow unattended, they become more difficult to uproot. Similarly, it's easier and less costly to uproot a seedling than to uproot a tree. Uprooting years of bitterness may require special equipment and out-of-pocket expenses. Thus, it's best to pull up the seed of bitterness early rather than allowing it to fester in your heart. Once we realize God is truly sovereign, we'll realize there's no need to remain bitter about the outcome of the relationship. We place everything in the mighty hands of God.

4. The Thorn of Self-Condemnation. Accepting God's will prevents me from questioning my self-worth. Rejection thrusts us in front of the mirror. We look at our reflection and ask, "What's wrong with me? Am I not smart enough? Am I not spiritually mature enough? Am I too fat? Am I too skinny?" We begin to condemn ourselves. We blame ourselves for something that may not have been our fault. It's amazing how we will experience rejection on a job interview, loan application, or housing contract and feel little impetus to make changes. Yet, there's something about romance that causes us to question our divine design and pursue change.

When we mistake God's sovereign will for unwarranted rejection, we attempt to make adjustments hoping to win someone else's acceptance. We change our wardrobe, enroll in fitness programs, and change our hairstyle. But when we make adjustments due to perceived rejection, our alterations are based on misinformation. Sometimes we may even ask the person, "What is it about me you don't like? Why won't you go out with me?" The other person may not even have the guts to tell you the honest truth, so they may make something up like, "I question your devotion to God. I'm looking for someone who prays more." Guess what you start doing? You double up on your prayer life! As far as God is concerned, He didn't have an issue with your prayer life! Don't get me wrong—I'm sure God won't mind the extra time with you. But accepting what God allows reminds me rejection does not mean there is something inherently wrong with me. We don't have to make any changes unless the Lord directs us to do so.

Here is one thing to keep in mind. The Mountain of Acceptance is a region that cannot be avoided along your journey through the wilderness. No matter how great the relationship is that you're leaving behind, take the lessons God intended to provide during your Seir experience and move onward.

KEVIN'S STORY

Kevin accepted Jesus Christ into his life when he was about thirteen years old. He wanted to meet and marry a Christian woman who was virtuous and faithful to God, but he found himself attracted to women who were the opposite. Although he found them physically attractive, they often didn't possess strong moral character. Kevin continuously fell in love with women who compromised their values and failed to walk uprightly before God. A series of blind dates and fruitless pursuits led him nowhere on his quest to find a godly mate. Further, many of the women he pursued did not share the same feelings. Kevin wondered if he would ever find the right woman.

This seemed to change when Kevin met Amanda. After spending time getting to know Amanda, she seemed to be the woman for Kevin. Unlike other women he dated, Amanda had a passion for God. She earnestly desired to please God and love Him more each day. Her passion for God's Word and ministry was evident to those around her. Kevin loved talking to her about scripture and the things of God. In addition, Amanda shared the same romantic feelings for Kevin as he did towards her.

The relationship continued to develop and they even met each other's families. Yet there was one thing missing—up to this point, their relationship was kept private. Kevin, however, was ready to make things "official." He wanted their relationship to go "public." He wanted the world to know about this brewing romance! When Kevin expressed this thought to Amanda, she was very hesitant. She told him she did not want to have a "public relationship." She also said she felt it was best if they simply remained friends.

Kevin was very disappointed. He knew what it meant to be rejected by ungodly women; even though his past rejections were difficult, he found the contrast of values with other women to be understandable. But now a godly woman was rejecting him. He said to himself, "Am I not good enough? Was it my family background? Did I not do or say the right things? Am I not worthy enough to be in a relationship with a Christian woman?" Though Kevin's relationship with Amanda was a mountain top experience, he had to embrace God's sovereignty. On The Mountain of Acceptance, he had to accept that Amanda was not the woman God had for him.

Even though Kevin understood God's sovereignty, he responded by drifting back to his old ways of dating. He started going out with women who did not make God a priority. He began lowering his standards in what he was looking for in a wife. He continuously ignored red flags. He said to himself, "No one's perfect. After all, she is a Christian. She does have a relationship with God."

During this phase he met Jennifer. Initially, Jennifer didn't seem to be passionate about the things of God. However, Kevin discovered they were still compatible in a lot of other areas—they enjoyed similar movies, shared a love for politics, enjoyed fruitful conversations, and came from similar backgrounds. In spite of this, Kevin continued to see red flags. Deep within, he felt he was compromising his standards and values. As the relationship progressed, Kevin fell more and more in love with Jennifer. His heart became attached to her. He felt a constant tug of war. Part of him enjoyed being with her, while the other part knew it was best to end the relationship. The longer he stayed in the relationship, the more difficult it was to leave.

Kevin asked himself a question that changed everything: "If she doesn't change another day in her life, would I be willing to spend the rest of my life with her?" Kevin immediately knew the answer was "no." At that moment Kevin decided to end the relationship. Even though Jennifer was a great person, he had to accept she was not who God had for him.

His descent from The Mountain of Acceptance was difficult. His conversation with Jennifer did not go well. He battled feelings of guilt. He even felt as if Jennifer gave him a guilt trip. She said to Kevin, "How could you do this to me?" At one point, she refused to believe Kevin truly meant it and figured he was going through a phase, forcing him to be very firm in communicating that the relationship was over.

Kevin was eventually able to move on through God's power and grace. Unfortunately, his relationships with Jennifer and Amanda have never been the same. Future encounters have been somewhat tense and uncomfortable. Kevin was disappointed that things didn't end the way he hoped. However, Kevin finds greater peace in knowing he embraced God's sovereignty on The Mountain of Acceptance.

LANDMARKS:

- The Mountain of Acceptance is where I must accept that a particular good thing is not intended for me.
- I must accept what God allows and embrace His sovereign will.
- The only way to leave The Mountain of Acceptance is to walk downhill.
- On The Mountain of Acceptance, I am assured of God's provision and presence.
- I must watch out for thorns of possession, deception, bitterness, and self-condemnation.

CHAPTER THREE

THE PLATEAU OF COMFORT

So we passed beyond our brothers the sons of Esau, who live in Seir, away from the Arabah road, away from Elath and from Ezion-geber. And we turned and passed through by the way of the wilderness of Moab. Then the Lord said to me, 'Do not harass Moab, nor provoke them to war, for I will not give you any of their land as a possession, because I have given Ar to the sons of Lot as a possession' (Deuteronomy 2:8-9).

The next stop on the Israelites' journey to Canaan was a city called Ar in a region called Moab. Ar consisted of a series of plateaus; high, flat terrain. The Moabites, descendants of Abraham's nephew Lot, inhabited this region. Once again, the Lord told Israel neither to take possession of the land nor provoke the inhabitants to war. As was the case on Mount Seir, God reserved this land for another nation of people, the Moabites.

WHAT'S COMFORTABLE

God's instructions to Israel grabbed my attention. Why would anyone even be tempted to settle in this wilderness? Why did God have to tell the Israelites not to possess the land? Wasn't forty years of wandering in the wilderness enough?

By this point most, if not all, of the generation that experienced slavery in Egypt had passed away. The new generation knew life only in the wilderness. Although they lived a nomadic life, the wilderness may have felt like "home." Of course, they heard about the Promised Land that was overflowing with milk and honey. They may have even envisioned it, but they never experienced it. Up to this point, the wilderness was their reality. It could have been easy and even tempting to settle for what they were already accustomed to.

The Plateau of Comfort is the land where we settle for a relationship or person because it's comfortable. It's the land of the familiar—our comfort zone. A relationship may be unhealthy. It may even cause us to regress spiritually. It may lack vitality. But it's comfortable. It's like remaining on a comfortable couch all day when we need to hop into our less comfortable desk chair to attend to our work. We prefer to stay on the couch rather than sit in the uncomfortable seat that yields progress. The same holds true when it comes to relationships.

The Plateau of Comfort may involve at least one of three things.

1. The Plateau of Comfort may involve a particular person. This may be someone you've dated for quite some time. This may the person with whom you're repeatedly "on again" and "off again." This is the person you've known since elementary school. This is the young lady you've been in love with since you met during freshman orientation.

These relationships thrive on history and tend to hold together based on a shared story. For instance, perhaps you had a memorable first encounter, or you've been through some difficult times together. So when the relationship is about to fall apart, each person reminisces about when they first met. They remember ten years ago when they looked into one another's eyes. Suddenly, the reality of their problems momentarily disappears.

As stressful, frustrating, or unhealthy as the relationship may be, they say, "We've been together for so long" or "We've been through a lot together." These relationships tend to go through a cycle of "break up and make up." Every time they break up, one person begins to feel very uncomfortable. He misses hearing her voice. She misses his company. So one person calls the other just to see "how they are doing." Before you know it, the two are back together.

Sometimes this cycle even persists amidst verbal and physical abuse. A physical confrontation or near-death experience leads to a temporary break up. Then the two people get back together and continue to go at each other's throats. They accept chaos as the norm. Unbelievably, this place is both harmful and comfortable at the same time.

2. *The Plateau of Comfort may involve a type of person.* Some people may not stay with the same person, but with the same type of person. They are constantly attracted to individuals with similar characteristics. They may even pat themselves on the back for getting out of an unhealthy relationship just to crawl right into another dysfunctional relationship with another person. Everyone hopes and prays each relationship will be different, but soon it's obvious he's no different than the guy she dated before or she treats him the same way his ex-girlfriend did. On The Plateau of Comfort, we settle for familiar traits and behaviors.

3. The Plateau of Comfort may involve a mindset or behavioral pattern. Sometimes, the way we think or behave keeps us stuck in the same place. I have had conversations with individuals who run into recurring relationship problems. I listen as they share their feelings and hurts. As these people talk, they eventually say something that provides insight into why they are drawn to the wrong individuals and drive away the type of people they really want. Some men say what they love about women. Some women say what they hate about men. They talk about what kind of person turns them off and gets them upset. They state their expectations in a relationship. They give a quick snapshot of their philosophy of romance.

There's a worldview that impacts their approach to relationships. When I detect an unhealthy mindset in one of these conversations, I try to address the relationship philosophy. Whenever a person gets defensive, I know that there's a problem. You cannot have a healthy relationship without abandoning unhealthy ways of thinking. The person who is stuck in The Plateau of Comfort will give his heart to individuals who fit his paradigm of right and wrong. He cannot experience relationships that go beyond this way of thinking.

In his book *21 Irrefutable Laws of Leadership*, John Maxwell discusses the Law of the Lid. Maxwell explains that one's leadership ability is the lid that determines how effective a leader will be. The lower an individual's ability to lead, the lower the lid will be on his or her potential. Conversely, the higher an individual's ability to lead, the higher the lid on his or her potential.

We also have a relationship lid. The kind of relationships we are able to handle and maintain is limited by our character and mindset. It is possible to want a healthy relationship, yet lack the integrity and spiritual fortitude to handle it. Furthermore, a person with a low relationship lid will frustrate and limit a partner who desires more. A "high lid" person who adheres to strong values, possesses praise-worthy character and handles responsibility well will eventually break up with a partner who has a low lid and lacks these desirable traits. We can either raise the lid and create more room for the right type of person, or find someone short enough to fit under the lid. If we choose The Plateau of Comfort as a settling place, we choose the latter.

CHARACTERISTICS OF THE PLATEAU

There are several things that tend to characterize The Plateau of Comfort. If you are facing one or more of these, you just may be in this territory.

1. Lack of Enthusiasm. On The Plateau of Comfort, one or both individuals experience diminished excitement about the relationship. There's no spark. Dates and conversations become monotonous. A longing to share one another's company is replaced with rote, obligatory encounters. If you are in this stage, you'll find yourself simply going through relational motions. The relationship feels more like duty than delight. As logical as it may seem to just pull out of the relationship, you know getting out is easier said than done. You may be afraid of hurting the other person's feelings. Just when you are ready to press the end button, familiarity trumps reason.

2. Lack of Spiritual Fervor. On The Plateau of Comfort, the relationship lacks spiritual fervor because God is not at the center of the relationship and you fail to encourage each other spiritually. It's possible for a couple to long to be in each other's presence, but not in God's presence. They may enjoy talking about everything, except Jesus Christ. They enjoy watching movies, but spend no time studying scripture together. God is not a priority in the relationship and decisions are made without seeking God's guidance or deferring to scripture. They may acknowledge that God brought them together. They may even attend a local church. However, that's the extent of their spiritual life. There's no deep intimacy with God.

Some couples may think it's okay to exclude Christ from their relationships. It may not seem like a big deal when you're dating, but it becomes a big deal in marriage. Marriage brings a level of complexity a couple doesn't experience during courtship. Both people have to take on responsibilities they didn't have to before and find themselves facing a new set of problems, conflicts, and trials. Many marriages crumble due to a weak spiritual foundation. Spiritual immaturity can only take you so far.

3. *Stagnancy.* On The Plateau of Comfort, the relationship can stagnate. Rather than deepening, the relationship remains on cruise control. The couple fails to learn anything new about each other. They may even struggle to spend time together.

A car stops when it runs out of gas, and a relationship stops when the couple stops growing. Ask yourself, "How much has our relationship grown over the past three months? Are we growing in the areas of communication, honor, and respect? Are we getting better at responding to challenges and resolving conflict? Are we growing closer together as friends?" Not only may the relationship stop, it may even go backwards. Maybe you begin to grow apart. The conversations become shorter. You spend less time together. Dishonor and disrespect become common. It becomes more and more difficult to communicate and resolve conflict. This type of relationship can keep you stuck.

On The Plateau of Comfort, not only do you experience a relational plateau, but your entire life plateaus. If we were to do an honest self-evaluation, we would realize crucial areas of our lives simultaneously flat line when we are in a plateaued relationship. Our spiritual fervor fizzles out. There's no movement when it comes to serving others. We put God-given assignments on hold and fail to develop our gifts. Important opportunities in our lives come to a standstill. You may have been on a steady climb prior to the relationship, growing and making progress. You were experiencing intimacy with God and seeing God accomplish amazing things in your life! But on this Plateau, the upward climb slowly flattened out.

4. *Lack of Vision.* You may be tempted to say, "Vision? Why do I need vision? I'm not trying to build an organization. I'm just trying to be in love!" The reality is every relationship needs a vision for where the relationship is going. Where there is no vision, people tend to wander around aimlessly from one situation to the next. Proverbs 29:18 says, "Where there is no vision, the people are unrestrained, but happy is he who keeps the law." Boundaries and values are tossed away when there's no apparent reason to keep them.

Some people possess relationship visions that lack quality. The things a couple envisions are neither healthy nor godly. In some cases a person envisions himself being married to a rich partner who will take care of his every need. Others have a good vision for a relationship, but often lose sight of it. When asked what they really desire in a relationship, they describe a relationship that is significantly different from the ones they are in.

One of my seminary professors often said, "As is, so then." In other words, a person will show you exactly who they are. You can't marry a person and then try to change him afterwards. You can't date a person who is irresponsible and expect that irresponsibility to vanish after saying "I do." When a person doesn't fit the vision God has given you for a healthy marriage, you may need the courage to let that person go. Rebelling against a God-given vision is a disaster waiting to happen.

It can be just as disastrous to move a relationship forward without seeking God for a clear vision. I think it's best to have a vision before entering a relationship. The clearer your vision, the better decisions you can make. You are more likely to make decisions based on scripture and conviction than romantic passion.

5. *Past Guilt.* Many of us have made mistakes that we are ashamed of. Too often we define ourselves by our past mistakes rather than our future potential. People who get stuck in The Plateau of Comfort may feel they deserve their relationship because they aren't worthy of anything better. A person who was once promiscuous may not feel worthy of someone who is committed to sexual purity. Someone who was a habitual liar may not feel that he can ever be in a relationship marked with honesty and trust. Someone who was once financially irresponsible may feel obligated to stay with someone who refuses to be a good steward of her resources.

But past failures do not disqualify you for future success. God forgives and heals.1 John 1:9 says, "If we confess our sins, He is faithful and righteous to forgive us our sins and to cleanse us from all unrighteousness." Psalm 103:12 tells us God removes our sins "as far as the east is from the west." If you repent, God starts you off on a clean slate. Your past is your past—don't allow it to define your present and your future. Being promiscuous in the past doesn't disqualify you from marrying a virgin now. Being a con artist in the past doesn't mean you must limit yourself to a dishonest spouse. The way to get off the plateaus is realizing God desires something much better for you.

As you move away from former habits and patterns, some may not accept your transformation or may think you're being a hypocrite. Your significant other may say to you, "How can you end the relationship when you have been guilty of the same things? Why can't you be more understanding?" You will have friends who won't be able to separate the new you from the old you. They won't be able to understand why you can't just stick it out with a person and embrace that person's toxic behavior. Their parents will believe you think you are "too good" to be with their son or daughter. There's no easy way around it. It's something that has to be done if you're going to move on. Once you make peace with your past, you can embrace a hopeful future.

6. *Mirages.* A mirage is an optical illusion. It is an image of a distant object, an image projected from a distance that is reflected as a reality in the current situation. You may see what appears to be a lake in a desert. As soon as you get excited for the opportunity to quench your thirst, you discover it's actually a body of water miles away.

Some people experience mirages in romantic relationships. They take the dreams, desires, and passion they have for a healthy relationship and project it onto the relationship they have. They believe a person has the love, godliness, and other desirable traits they want, but it's a mirage. Their honest, trustworthy boyfriend is actually deceitful. The fiancé who appears loving, kind, and sweet lacks kindness and unconditional love. When you mistake a mirage for reality, you don't fall in love with the actual person. You fall in love with your perception of the person. You are in love with a fantasy that doesn't really exist.

A mirage can develop when two people aren't able to spend sufficient time with each other. It becomes easy to formulate an image in one's mind to compensate for the lack of physical interaction. Even couples who become married after a long-distance relationship may discover that some of the things they thought they loved about the other person weren't real.

Sometimes, the mirage may be the result of former characteristics that no longer exist.

Maybe the person you adore was once godly, respectful, and generous. Yet, for some reason, those characteristics are no longer present. You refuse to believe that the traits you once admired have vanished. It's easier and more comfortable to pretend they are there than to admit they are not.

A mirage is developed in the realm of fantasy. Whenever there's a gap between reality and a perceived ideal or the unknown, we tend to fill that gap with fantasy. The reality may be that the person does not possess noble character or compassion, but our perceived ideal may be to have someone with those characteristics. We then fill the gap by conjuring up an image of the person that isn't true. Likewise, if there are things about a person that remain unknown, we fill in the blanks in our fantasy world. Our fantasy then causes us to lose focus on reality.

This is why we need people around us who can see clearly. These people can tell if we are seeing a mirage. They know a lake when they see one! Rather than succumbing to our own projections, the best thing we can do is to listen to trustworthy individuals who see what we're unable to see.

WHITE ELEPHANTS

On The Plateau of Comfort, we encounter issues we prefer to ignore than to address. For instance, it may be obvious the relationship is not be working out. Rather than sitting down to have a difficult conversation, we allow the relationship to continue. On The Plateau of Comfort, we abandon courage to make difficult decisions. We delude ourselves into thinking we're looking out for the other person. The reality is we simply lack courage to face the aftermath of difficult decisions and we're just delaying the inevitable. It's more comfortable to let things stay the way they are than rock the boat with the truth.

For this reason, couples remain together long after they should have called it quits. It's similar to using a product beyond its expiration date. There are clear warnings that the product is no longer safe to use. Likewise, some relationships have an expiration date. The same relationship that may have been pleasurable before is now emotionally toxic. What may have seemed to be a source of life begins to drain you. You see the unhealthy side effects of prolonged use. Yet, you ignore the problems and continue in the relationship.

UNCOMFORTABLE COMFORT

Once we recognize we are on a relational plateau, this comfortable terrain will become increasingly uncomfortable. At some point, you become tired of The Plateau of Comfort and realize you want a productive life and fruitful relationships. Like the person who has spent most of his day on the comfortable couch, casually hanging out begins to feel like a waste of time.

A growing relationship with Christ may hasten this process. As you grow in Christ and truly begin to yearn for Him, you will begin to desire more. Moreover, as you spend time studying God's Word, you will discover God's vision for your life and relationships. As you're filled with the Spirit, you are energized to move forward to better terrain. You share an experience similar to the Israelites. Even though the Israelites were on a plateau that may have seemed like good land, God described a better future home:

For the Lord your God is bringing you into a good land, a land of brooks of water, of fountains and springs, flowing forth in valleys and hills; a land of wheat and barley, of vines and fig trees and pomegranates, a land of olive oil and honey; a land where you will eat food without scarcity, in which you will not lack anything; a land whose stones are iron, and out of whose hills you dig copper. When you have eaten and are satisfied, you shall bless the Lord your God for the good land which He has given you (Deuteronomy 8:7-10).

God was leading the Israelites to a prosperous land, a land flowing with milk and honey. He was not taking them to a desolate land with sparse vegetation and dried-up streams. Rather, He set aside a place of rich vegetation and abundant resources. The Israelites would prosper in the good land, and rightly give praise to God for the bountiful blessing.

God wants to bless us, and we need a vision of the good God has in store. God wants what's best for you. He wants a relationship marked with integrity and purity. He wants you to experience joy and growth. He wants your mate to be someone who will love, honor, cherish, and respect you. He wants a person who is willing to sacrifice for you and help you be all God is calling you to be. He wants you to have a suitable helper who is an asset, not a liability. Yet, it is important you have a vision for it. You must develop a mental picture of the type of marriage God wants for you. Once you have a clear vision, you can make good decisions. But if you don't have a promised land-vision, you will settle for the rocks and shrubs of the wilderness.

DON'T SETTLE

If you find yourself on The Plateau of Comfort, here is the biggest thing you have to remember: don't settle! Don't settle for a person because it's comfortable. Don't embrace a relationship because it's what you are familiar with. Don't hold on to a mindset because it's always been your mode of survival. True, you may have known each other for years. You may have weathered storms together. Yes, your families are intertwined. I know that you've been in love since junior high school. I know your mother adores her. Nevertheless, you deserve better. God has so much more in store for you. There is a God who is able to do exceedingly, abundantly, and far above all that you could ask, think, or imagine.

I would like to take a few moments to talk to the men. Proverbs 18:22 says that a man who finds a wife finds a good thing and obtains favor from the Lord. Notice that the verse didn't say an average thing, but a good thing. A man ought to look for a good, godly woman. He is to find a woman of excellence. Proverbs 31:29 says, "Many daughters have done nobly, but you excel them all." I believe every man should be able to say this about his future wife. If you cannot look a potential mate in her eyes and say this verse, keep looking. No future wife of yours should be number ten or number thirty-three on the list of godly women you admire. She shouldn't even be first on the list. She should be in a category of her own. She should feel like your promised land.

To the ladies, take your time and wait for a man of valor and virtue. You too should desire to have an excellent spouse. Even though many women look towards Proverbs 31 to identify the type of wife they should aspire to be, it was actually written for men! It was the advice of King Lamuel's mother on what he should be looking for in a woman. Interestingly, the first nine verses address the characteristics of an honorable man. Your future husband shouldn't be the man who is captivated by money, women, and alcohol. He is to be a man of integrity and justice. You need a godly man who serves others and who can lead your future family. You need a man to whom you can comfortably say, "I'm willing to follow your leadership." Once you marry a man, he immediately becomes the head of the household. It's possible for one to be a leader by position and not by practice. The question you must ask yourself is, "Do I feel comfortable and confident with his style of leadership?" The man you choose to marry should feel like your promised land.

Keep in mind that a decision not to settle goes beyond your interaction with a significant other. Attraction is not just about finding or meeting the right type of person. It's about being the right type of person. In order to be a suitable mate, you must abandon areas of comfort and complacency in your own conduct and strive to be all God is calling you to be. Life is not about sitting on a couch waiting to meet the love of your life. You must first pursue God. You must make God your number one passion. Maximize every moment you have to walk in your God-given purpose. Be the servant God has called you to be. Strive to grow. Leave the comfortable couch and attend to areas of brokenness in your life. As much as possible, strive to be whole. A companion may help you, but only Christ can complete you.

LEONARD'S STORY

Leonard comes from a family of military men. Both his father and grandfather served in the United States military and he followed suit by enlisting in the Air Force. As he grew up, Leonard's parents only attended church sporadically. During one of those occasions, when he was 13, Leonard accepted Jesus Christ into his life. But as Leonard got older, he strayed away from the things of God largely due to the influence of his peers. These friends also influenced the kind of women he dated.

During his Air Force training, Leonard met Merlinda in one of his classes. Merlinda and Leonard hit it off almost instantly. In many ways, Merlinda felt like a "younger sister" to Leonard. They grew more familiar with each other through a study group and it became apparent to Leonard that Merlinda was developing deeper feelings for him. However, Leonard wasn't quite sure if he felt the same way.

As always, Leonard's peers began to influence his decision. They thought he should begin dating Merlinda and see what happened. After all, Merlinda was intelligent, compassionate, and fun. They thought Leonard would be crazy not to give an amazing woman like Merlinda a chance. Leonard decided to give the relationship a shot.

However, as time progressed, Leonard discovered his feelings towards Merlinda were not changing. Yet, Merlinda continued to "pursue him." She took the initiative to make sure dates happened. She went out of her way to make sure they spent time together. She seemed to be happy just to have a moment of his time. Even though Leonard wasn't in love with Merlinda, she provided a sense of companionship and it was easy to let the relationship happen.

After almost a year and half, Leonard grew uncomfortable with this attitude and knew he had to end the relationship. One day, Leonard was honest with Merlinda and said it was not fair to her to be in a one-sided relationship. Like most break-up conversations, their conversation was not easy, but Leonard knew the only path to liberty was being honest. He realized he would have to trust God to provide his future mate.

Leonard eventually met another young lady. Unlike Merlinda, she moved him. Her godliness and beauty captivated him. Instead of being pursued by Merlinda, Leonard took the leadership and pursued this young lady. Whereas Merlinda initially showed interest in spiritual things because of Leonard, this young lady pursued and served God on her own. After a year of friendship and courtship, Leonard proposed to her and they are now making plans to be married. Leonard's defining moment came when he decided he was not going to settle on The Plateau of Comfort.

LANDMARKS:

- The Plateau of Comfort is identified as the land where I settle for a relationship or person because it's comfortable.
- The Plateau of Comfort may involve a particular person, type of person, mindset, or behavioral pattern.
- I must pay attention to the signs that indicate that I'm on The Plateau of Comfort.
- As I grow, I become uncomfortable with being comfortable.
- Don't settle on The Plateau of Comfort.

CHAPTER FOUR
THE VALLEY OF ONE

> *"Now arise and cross over the brook Zered yourselves." So we crossed over the brook Zered. Now the time that it took for us to come from Kadesh-barnea until we crossed over the brook Zered was thirty-eight years, until all the generation of the men of war perished from within the camp, as the Lord had sworn to them. Moreover the hand of the Lord was against them, to destroy them from within the camp until they all perished.*
>
> Deuteronomy 2:13-15

In Deuteronomy 2 we find the Israelites preparing to cross the Zered Valley. The crossing of the valley marked an end of an era for Israel, a time when they finished their wilderness journey and prepared for the promised land. By this point, the entire generation, except for Joshua and Caleb, that originally refused to enter Canaan had already died. Also, the Zered Valley was the only place along the journey where Israel had no interaction with other nations. There were no merchants from which to purchase items. There was no monetary exchange. There was no communication with second parties. It was just them and God.

This is what I call The Valley of One. The Valley of One is where you have no romantic relationship with anyone. No one is calling you and you have no one to call. Your weekends are filled with dateless nights. Relationships with the opposite sex are platonic. Even if there's someone you have feelings for, romantic involvement is a long shot. In The Valley of One, it's just you and God.

The Valley of One is also a place of purging. In the same way God purged the old generation and replaced it with the new, God purges our old habits and replaces them with new ones. For many it's a place of transition. It's where God prepares us for something He may have in the future, which may (or may not) include marriage.

The Valley of One is a low place. Out of all the terrains, the valley is probably the lowest in elevation. It is can be dark and lonely. Your days in the valley will be filled with disappointment and your nights will be filled with tears. In Psalm 23, the psalmist David refers to his situation as "the valley of the shadow of death." You will be tempted to make unwise and unhealthy decisions in the valley. But in the same Psalm, David said God would be with him in the valley. The Valley of One is where you are assured of God's presence in your life and He invites you to commune with Him.

The Valley of One is where God wants to have your undivided attention and devotion without the distraction of a romantic relationship. Of course, there's nothing wrong with being in this kind of relationship, but there are times in our lives where God chooses something different for us.

He tends to do this two ways:

1. He closes doors. You will pursue relationships but things won't work out. It will frustrate you when God doesn't seem to create opportunities for you to be with someone. Isaiah 22:22 and Revelation 3:7-8 teach that God opens doors no one can close and closes doors that no one can open. This, my friend, includes you. God will close relational doors that you won't be able open. You will be tempted to pry open a closed door, chasing after someone who's not interested or isn't best for you.

But the valley is designed for you to travel alone, just you and your Savior. In this stage, three is a crowd. Of course, I'm not speaking about friendships, family, accountability, and small groups. We need community especially at this time. But in The Valley of One, there is no romantic love.

2. He nudges you. You may be presented with an offer to be in a relationship. At first you may even see it as a God-granted moment. However, you will feel the Spirit of God nudging you not to proceed. As much as you desire to move forward, you feel God pulling you back. He will reveal to you through His Word, other people, and life situations that this is not the season for you to be romantically involved with anyone. If this is the case for you, do not quench the Spirit.

RUSHING THROUGH THE VALLEY

As a single person, your tendency will be to rush through The Valley of One. You will yearn for the day to when you no longer have to be alone and you will be tempted to see this stage as a curse. However, The Valley of One is actually a blessing. It is an opportunity for you to draw closer to God than you ever have before. If you someday marry, it will be difficult to have The Valley of One experience with God, but during this season you can spend hours in prayer without the interruption of children and a spouse. You will be able to serve and give back to the community any time you choose, but when you get married, you will have other responsibilities to consider.

Some people simply endure this stage. They just suffer and wait for someone to sweep them off their feet. They may even spend most of their days complaining and whining about not being in a relationship. If it were not for the sovereignty of God, they would not choose to be in The Valley of One. They see it as being drafted into war against their will.

Others cheat their way through The Valley of One. They find a "companion" whose friendship has elements of romance, but they don't truly want to be with that person. They want companionship without commitment. The person is used to fill an emotional and social void. Being with the person feels better than being alone. It validates our self-worth and self-esteem. Even though we aren't in love with the person, we're in love with the fact that someone is in love with us. This kind of relationship is like having counterfeit money—it gives you the feeling of having something real, but it has no value. The relationship has the appearance of romance, but you're simply delaying the inevitable. This type of situation always leaves someone hurt, and it also robs us of valuable time in which God could have had more focused attention.

Some people find "companionship" in unhealthy things such as pornography, alcohol, drugs, and workaholism. Instead of finding solace in Christ, they find something else to date. The bottle becomes their lover. A website becomes their fiancé. They begin dating their job or a project.

BEING ALONE

In moments of being alone, we may feel as if God has left us. Intellectually, we may know He's omnipresent, but emotionally He's omni-nowhere. David felt the same way as he poured out his heart in Psalm 13. Listen to what he says:

> *How long, O Lord? Will You forget me forever?*
> *How long will you hide Your face from me?*
> *How long shall I take counsel in my soul, having sorrow*
> *in my heart all the day?*

In Psalm 10, he also says, "Why do you stand afar off, O Lord? Why do You hide Yourself in times of trouble?"

In The Valley of One, you may feel like God has forgotten about you or He is ignoring you. It will feel as if all of heaven is on vacation. However, God has not left you. In fact, when God seems the farthest away is often when He's closest. God is at work, even when He appears to be silent.

One of the biggest temptations in The Valley of One is to have a spirit of murmuring. We can complain about the person we don't have and remain oblivious to the many things we do have. Complaining robs our spirit of gratitude and thanksgiving. Deep inside, we hope our complaining will urge God to hurry things along and send us a mate. It's sort of like the little child who cries and whines because she can't have her toy. She fusses until her frazzled parents finally give in.

But God is not going to place a rush order on a spouse because we feel we need one by the end of the year. Our murmuring is a sign that we aren't truly prepared. The Israelites murmured and complained in the wilderness. Yet, this attitude did not accelerate their journey to the Promised Land. If anything, it played a role in prolonging it. At the root of our murmuring is selfishness. We are not excited that things aren't going our way. We can't understand why the Sovereign God of the universe won't adjust His will to fit ours. Our prayers are, "Lord, not Your will, but mine be done."

Murmuring is also a sign of discontent. We still believe that a person will fill that empty void in our lives. However, if we are discontent when we are single, we will be discontent when we are married. No person is designed to fill our deepest longing.

REVENGE ROMANCE

In The Valley of One, we will be tempted to develop a relationship with someone out of a spirit of revenge. We may do it to get back at someone who has hurt us, or to prove to an ex that we are still capable of finding someone. We may even seek revenge romance against God because we feel as if God has disappointed us. We say, "OK, Lord. Since you're not sending anyone my way, I'll just have to take matters into my own hands. If I just happen to marry an unbeliever or serial killer, it will be completely Your fault."

If this is something you're struggling with, I want to encourage you with this story. In Numbers 14, the Israelites realized they made a huge mistake by not seizing the Promised Land as God had commanded. God told them, "Since you will not take possession of the land, you will spend 40 years wandering in the wilderness. One year represented each day that you spied out the wilderness, but still did not trust me. As a matter of fact, this entire generation will die out and I will raise up a new generation to seize the Promised Land."

Understandably, the Israelites quickly had a change of mind. The next morning, the camp came to Moses and said, "After sleeping on it, we realized we have sinned and have decided to go up and seize the land like God said." What was Moses' response? "This will not succeed! Do not go up, because the LORD is not with you. You will be defeated by your enemies!"

Here's my encouragement to you. If you are thinking about dating, proposing to, or marrying somebody out of anger towards God, it will not work. God will not be with you. This is not to say that you won't have His presence. You simply won't have His favor. A relationship with rebellion as its foundation is sure to crumble. Marriage will not erase the problems in that relationship—it will magnify them!

REBOUND ROMANCE

Another type of relationship you'll be tempted to enter is similar to a revenge romance. It's called rebound romance. Whereas revenge relationships are meant to hurt someone else, rebound relationships are meant to prove something to oneself, to fill an emotional void or prove to ourselves we are still worthy of love. Because many people base their self-worth on whether or not someone likes and accepts them, the thought of being without a relationship is downright terrifying!

However, people who bounce from relationship to relationship because they are afraid to be alone never truly learn how to depend on God. God never becomes their all and all. When these individuals enter into marriage, they either look to their spouse to be everything to them or they never know how to trust God in dealing with life's challenges.

Some married Christian couples decide they need to separate. Sometimes, I can't help but wonder—should they have separated while they were dating? Maybe they should have taken some time to be alone and allow their relationship with God to deepen. Maybe they would have held each other's hands tighter in marriage if they learned to hold on to God's hand tighter while they were single.

HOW LONG?

God determines your duration in The Valley of One. For some people, it's a short journey. For others, it's long. At least God told the Israelites they would wander in the wilderness for 40 years. Joshua and Caleb had the opportunity to count the days. However, God doesn't tell us how long we will journey through The Valley of One.

There are some things you have to consider during your time in the valley:

1. *The longer you stay, the more uncomfortable others feel.* Some people in your life will begin to think something is wrong with you because you are still single. Anxious parents will pressure you for grandchildren. Friends will tell you your standards are too high. Acquaintances may even question your sexual orientation. Don't allow the pressure of others to force you into a relationship that's not the best for you. It is better to be single and lonely than married and miserable.

2. *The longer you stay, the more set in your ways you become.* This is probably the biggest drawback to being in the valley; you develop habits and a way of life that becomes a comfort zone for you. When you become married, you'll discover you may have to make adjustments in areas where you have become settled. As you are single, realize that a future marriage will require making

sacrifices. Enjoy everything about being single, but realize you may have to adjust or even get rid of some of those things in marriage.

3. *The longer you stay, the more impatient you will become.* It is difficult not to look at the clock and watch the time pass away. You'll be tempted to lower your standards and compromise your values out of impatience. When you first enter a store, you desire to have a certain standard of service. After waiting for several hours, you come to a point where you simply want someone to serve you. You'll begin looking for shortcuts to speed up the relationship process. Unfortunately, taking a short cut can lead to major setbacks.

Some people believe The Valley of One is simply a preparation place for marriage, but The Valley of One is not a holding cell. It's a place where God seeks to be Lord in our lives on a greater level.

In fact, for some people The Valley of One will be their final destination. For whatever reason, God chooses or allows some people to remain single. For a variety of reasons, this is where some people will camp out and spend the rest of their lives.

This seems abnormal in our romance-driven culture. This seems abnormal in our romance-driven churches! We sometimes have a sense of entitlement that God "owes" us a mate. We assume God will give us a mate and all we have to do is wait until he or she comes, but this is not always the case. Whether because of a special calling from God, a series of circumstances, or a personal choice, some people will remain in the valley.

MAXIMIZE YOUR SINGLENESS

In The Valley of One, maximize your singleness. Live your life to the full! Serve God with all your heart! Pursue God's calling for your life. Give yourself back to humanity.

Always remember Jesus was single, yet He modeled what it meant to live life to the full. Jesus healed the sick, raised the dead, touched the broken, and preached the gospel. He came to earth to do one thing—to fulfill the will of the Father. Through this fulfilling, He had fulfillment. If The Valley of One is to be your last stop, you can live a fulfilled life. You can spend the rest of your life serving God and others. You can devote your life to missions, discipling others, and doing what God calls you to do.

In 1 Corinthians 7, Paul talks about the benefits of the single life. He uses the term "undistracted devotion." This means being able to give one's self fully to God and His work without the distraction of a marriage.

Paul wasn't saying marriage forces a person to be worldly and fleshly. No pastor who is conducting a wedding will say, "Today marks the beginning of a beautiful marriage and the end of your relationship with God!" Married people simply have to be concerned about things in this life that may not have been as urgent when they were single: life insurance, keeping up a home, taking care of children, and other concerns. In addition, they must take into account how they may please and honor their spouse on a daily basis.

The single person, however, has more time to focus on the things of God and give large amounts of time, energy, and resources to God's kingdom. A single person may be able to go on an international mission trip at a moment's notice. A married person has to consider her family and if the timing is right with her spouse. A single person can clean out his bank account and give it to someone in need. A married person has to consider the needs of his spouse, family, and related financial responsibilities. Single people can take bold steps of faith. Married people may have to slow down on making those same steps if their spouse is uncomfortable.

However, instead of focusing on the Lord and how to please Him, single people often focus on the things of the world and how to please a spouse that doesn't even exist! Time, energy, and focus that could be going to God and His work is spent worrying about who we will marry. We are more consumed with pursuing a relationship with a man than a relationship with the One who made man.

Married people who didn't maximize their singleness may then try to play "catch up" in marriage. Instead of focusing on their spouse, they try to serve God as if they were still single. They suddenly want to devote all their time, energy, and efforts into the Lord's work. They volunteer for organizations, spearhead initiatives, and give away large sums of money. These things are not bad in and of themselves; the challenge comes when these things begin to interfere with the marriage because the spouse begins to feel neglected or the children begin to feel mommy and daddy love ministry more than them.

This is what Paul warns us about. Basically he's saying, "Marriage is a beautiful thing! If God has marriage in the future for you, go for it! If you see someone you desire to marry, pursue it! However, I just want to give you a heads up. Realize that marriage requires a new set of priorities. You may not be able to devote the same amount of time to the work of God as you did while you were single."

This is the beauty of The Valley of One. You can maximize your singleness by giving yourself completely to God and His work. If you get married some day, you'll be able to look back at your single days without regret. You'll be able to tell stories of the great things God did in and through you a single person.

When I was single in college, I made up my mind that I was going to be content with being single and maximize my singleness. I prayed and believed that God would send me a mate, but in the meantime, I would just keep serving Him. I went to seminary and went on my first mission trip, a 10-week journey to eight islands by myself. Whenever I had an opportunity to learn about marriage, I took it. I attended seminars, Bible studies, and conferences and retreats. I read books and got equipped. There were times I became impatient. There were lonely times. Some days were dark, but I was determined to devote myself to God and His work. If this ended up being my last stop on the journey, I would have lived a fulfilled life.

This is an example of how my life has changed since singlehood:

SINGLE	MARRIED
Made a final decision on a mission trip at short notice.	Went on a mission trip after careful thought and planning with my spouse.
My financial decisions affected me.	My financial decisions affect our entire family.
Did ministry work at any time of day or night.	Set boundaries on when I devote my time to ministry.
Gave of my time freely.	Schedule and protect time with my family.

SINGLE	MARRIED
Took high risks with little planning.	Take risks with much planning and affirmation from spouse.
Said "yes" to most invitations.	Say "no" to some invitations.
Came home whenever I desired.	Call home when I'm running late.
Attended conferences and seminars.	Limit my conference and seminar attendance.

After graduating from seminary, a friend and I both felt God was calling us to move back to the same city. As a single person at the time, I told him I was just going to step out on faith. I was going to trust God to provide my need. He said, "That's awesome, Jumaine. For me, I can't just jump up and move like that. I have to consider my wife. Plus, my kids are still in school. We have to look at things financially." Were his concerns about worldly matters and pleasing his spouse? Absolutely. He and his family did eventually step out on faith and made the move, but it took them more time and consideration.

Living in The Valley of One is like living life through binoculars. Every so often, you have to refocus the lens. Life will be filled with blurred days. You will get distracted. You will become disgruntled. You will be lonely. You will question God only to receive no answers from heaven. You may feel your heart drifting towards the wrong type of person. However, you have to refocus the lens. Don't travel with blurred vision. Allow God to refocus the vision that He has for your life.

A few years ago, I ran into a pastor at a youth event. We attended the same seminary, but had never met. During our conversation, we talked a bit about how God was using us. At the time, I was praying about starting a church. He had been pastoring for a few years and had an itinerary that took him around the country. The conversation then drifted towards marriage. I shared that I had been married for about a year. He said, "Yeah, I'm still single." I told him that God would provide in His time, and began praying God would provide him with a wife. Several years went by. He continued to pastor, preach around the country, and touch lives. We even encouraged each other as I went on to start a church and he continued to see his young church grow and expand. God used him as a single man.

One Sunday, I found out he passed away. I was completely shocked. I couldn't believe he died at such a young age and in the prime of his ministry. Long after his passing, people continued posting comments on his Facebook page about how much he impacted their lives.

What if he had decided to place his life on hold until marriage? What if he had decided he wasn't going to maximize his singleness? For him, The Valley of One was the final stop. Yet, his journey alone did not stop him from giving his life to God and to His work. He maximized his singleness.

THOMAS'S STORY

Thomas was born and raised in the city and his parents often took him to church. When Thomas was nine years old, he placed his faith in Jesus Christ. Although he did not always make wise decisions, he continued to hold fast to his faith in Jesus as he got older. Unlike other boys who took a light perspective on relationships, Thomas always wanted to find a serious relationship that would end in marriage. He didn't have many girlfriends, but was serious about those he did date. In addition, he chose to have relationships with girls who also had faith in Jesus Christ.

A pivotal point in Thomas' life came as a freshman in college when his mother passed away after a battle with cancer. As a committed mother, she often placed her family's needs before her own. Her dream to one day develop a community center never came to fruition as she instead chose to focus on raising her children. Thomas was determined to have a wife like his mother who reflected godly attributes and virtues. He wanted to feel God's leading in anyone with whom he pursued a relationship. But unlike his mom, he didn't want to die with his dreams. He wanted to fulfill anything God had called him to.

His pursuit for a wife was not without disappointment. In one relationship, he discovered the young woman struggled with her faith in God and was confused as to what she truly believed. There was another young lady he sincerely loved, but she did not have the same feelings towards him. After a year of pursuing her, Thomas had to leave The Mountain of Acceptance.

Thomas's friends encouraged him to lower his standards, saying, "You're too picky! The type of woman you are looking for is unrealistic! She doesn't exist!"

Despite these challenges, Thomas decided not to put his life on hold. He was not going to mope around and complain about not having a wife. He made a commitment to maximize his singleness. He took advantage of an opportunity to work for a major recording artist. He began leading worship at various churches and started writing his own music. Some of his songs were even featured on major recording projects. He also developed a heart for missions and went on several mission trips. He seized opportunities to serve others and help people who were in need. His alone time was spent growing in God's Word and deepening his relationship with Him.

And he continued to look for the person God had for him. He met a young lady at church who did not share the same standards of sexual purity as Thomas did. Thomas continued in the relationship hoping things would change, but one night he found himself in a compromising position and he gave into sexual temptation. He couldn't believe it. After years of remaining pure, he allowed himself to give in. Thomas repented before God and sought His forgiveness. He recommitted himself to sexual purity and continued to pursue God.

After years of waiting and serving God, Thomas now believes God has sent the right person into his life. The lady his friends said did not exist is now here! As the relationship continues, Thomas continues to be prayerful. If this relationship does lead to marriage, he'll be able to reflect and be thankful that he maximized his singleness in The Valley of One.

LANDMARKS

- The Valley of One is where God desires to have my undivided attention and devotion without the distraction of a romantic relationship.
- If I am discontent when I'm single, I will be discontent when I'm married.
- No one is created to fulfill my deepest longing.
- I must be careful of the temptations of revenge and rebound romance, as well as murmuring and complaining.
- In The Valley of One, I must maximize my singleness.

CHAPTER FIVE

THE WILDERNESS OF SPECTATING

> *Today you shall cross over Ar, the border of Moab. When you come opposite the sons of Ammon, do not harass them nor provoke them, for I will not give you any of the land of the sons of Ammon as a possession, because I have given it to the sons of Lot as a possession.*
>
> *Deuteronomy 2:18-19*

The Israelites' journey continued. God told Moses they would depart Moab crossing the border at Ar and would enter land belonging to the descendants of Ammon. Like Moab, Ben-ammi (the progenitor of the Ammonites) was one of Lot's sons. (You can read the jaw dropping account of their conception in Genesis 19.) God informed Israel this land was given to the Ammonites. Can you imagine how the people felt as they repeatedly heard God say the land was set aside for other groups? Not only did Esau's descendants receive land, but also Lot's descendants …two different regions for each of his sons!

A similar scenario plays out in relationship journeys. If this were a relationship, it would be the third letdown, the third encounter that led to no meaningful relationship. I'm sure some of us have been there. By this point, we are emotionally drained and even spiritually disillusioned. Our faith in God begins to waiver. We lose confidence in God's ability to meet our needs and satisfy our natural desires. We begin to wonder if He is truly trustworthy. Although God continues to provide in other areas of our lives, we question His ability to provide companionship. We sound like the psalmist David in Psalm 77:7-9: "Will the Lord reject us forever? Will He never show His favor again? Has His unfailing love vanished forever? Has His promise failed for all time? Has God forgotten to be merciful? Has He in anger withheld his compassion?"

LIFE OF A SPECTATOR

This stage of the journey is called The Wilderness of Spectating, because it's where you watch God provide for everyone except you. Everyone else appears to be reaching their promised land and experiencing relationship bliss; your friends are getting married, having children, and buying new homes. All the students on your college campus seem to be in a dating relationship. Your roommates all have dates every weekend. Meanwhile, the guys swoon over all the girls in your circle except you, or you feel left out as women inquire about your friends yet express no interest in you.

It seems like everyone else gets a shot to play in the championships. Some even come home with a MVP trophy! All the while, you sit on the sidelines watching.

There are several characteristics that mark a spectator. All spectators should be aware of these hazards that exist on the sidelines.

1. Spectators tend to measure their self-worth based on who's in the game. Spectators feel as if they are not good enough to play—after all, if they were, they would have been picked. Many people buy into a scarcity mentality that success for someone else means failure for them. They see a friend entering into a dating relationship as one less opportunity for them. A friend getting married is a reminder that they will be going home to an empty house. Even though they smile on the outside, resentment, frustration, or sadness wells up within.

2. Spectators tend to react and take matters into their own hands. After a while the spectator says, "Well, if no one is going to let me play, I will start my own game." This is not only true in dating, but in life. People get tired of not having an opportunity to preach or teach, so they start a church. Instead of making improvements recommended by a supervisor, the employee quits and tries to start her own company. Instead of waiting on God, a person launches out and tries to get in a relationship in his own strength. Spectators begin to compromise their values in order to attract someone. They say "yes" in circumstances where they would typically say "no." They can end up trying to force things, wanting to pry open a locked door. Instead of seeking to move where the wind of God's Spirit may be blowing, they try to create movement.

3. Spectators can become jealous and envious. When romance becomes a god, the person who worships it becomes jealous of those who attain it. They begin to resent and even cut off relationships with their friends. I've witnessed this far too many times, like the bridesmaid who becomes increasingly jealous of the bride and causes conflict over petty issues. If the friendship survives the wedding ceremony the friend hurls unpleasant comments at the new couple and eventually drifts away.

If the root of bitterness remains, the spectator is likely to become jealous of anyone who is in a relationship, even friends and family members.

4. Spectators can feel like victims. They may feel as if they are being singled out, as if there is some sort of conspiracy to prevent them from being in a romantic relationship. They regard romance as a blessing and being single or alone as a curse. They begin to see people and even God as their enemies. They think God and other people have gotten in the way of the love they so earnestly desire or they say no one loves or cares about them.

These spectators fail to realize that not being in a romantic relationship is neither a tragedy nor a curse. Being alone isn't an offense that must be corrected, and they are not victims. God's lovingkindness extends to them although they may not fully recognize it.

5. Spectators can develop a sense of entitlement. Spectators may feel as if God owes them a romantic relationship. They say, "I've attended church services. I've fed the poor. I've given financially to You and others. I've made sacrifices. The only thing I ask is for you to give me someone to love and You're not making it happen!" A sense of entitlement causes us to draw incorrect conclusions and place misguided expectations on God. It makes us feel that life has ripped us off and we need to issue ultimatums: if God doesn't meet specific conditions, He must not be as loving and faithful as He claims to be.

The prodigal son's brother exhibits the same behavior in Luke 15. Because he was an obedient son, for whom the father never threw an elaborate party, the brother resented the celebration when the prodigal son returned home. The eldest son said, "'Look! For so many years I have been serving you and I have never neglected a command of yours; and yet you have never given me a young goat, so that I might celebrate with my friends; but when this son of yours came, who has devoured your wealth with prostitutes, you killed the fattened calf for him" (Luke 15:29-30). The eldest son had a sense of entitlement that prevented him from celebrating his brother's return. He was unable able to enjoy the moment and celebrate his brother's return because he was focusing on his own desires.

6. *Spectators feel left out.* This is probably the deepest emotional feeling in The Wilderness of Spectating. Spectators can't help but think they are missing out on something special. It seems like everyone has been invited to the party except them.

LEARNING TO CELEBRATE

In The Wilderness of Spectating, it is vital to celebrate others. If someone has met the person God has for him or her, we ought to rejoice. If a loved one is getting married, we should be happy and supportive.

Romans 12:15 says, "Rejoice with those who rejoice, and weep with those who weep." Verse 16 goes on to encourage us to live in harmony with one another. Of course, there are people who rejoice over evil and bad decisions. The scripture doesn't mean we are to rejoice with others regardless of the circumstance. If someone rejoices because they got away with robbing a bank, that's no cause to celebrate! However, when God is truly working in someone's life, we ought to rejoice with him. Likewise, when the hearts of our loved ones are sorrowful, we should enter into their sorrow by letting them know they are not alone.

The spectator often responds to circumstances the opposite

way; rather than rejoicing with someone, she secretly weeps over her own circumstances. Instead of weeping in response to another's misfortune, he inwardly rejoices knowing his misery has company.

Celebrating others not only allows others to feel loved—it also does a work in us, preventing our hearts from becoming bitter, resentful, and angry. It reminds us God is still faithful and He is able to provide for us in His timing. Celebrating others reminds us life is bigger than the situation that we face. Celebrating others allows us to reflect the love and glory of God to others.

Some may question how it's possible for the distraught spectator to genuinely celebrate. You may be asking, "What if my heart isn't in it? What if I don't feel like celebrating? Doesn't that mean I'm being fake?" Here is something to keep in mind.

Sometimes we have to do the right thing, even though we may not feel like it at the time. Remember when you were a child? You didn't always feel like doing everything your parents asked you to do. They may have told you to eat your vegetables when you wanted to skip right to dessert. You didn't feel like cleaning your room, but it was necessary to keep your room organized. Now that you're an adult, you find yourself doing the very things you refused to do as a child. You cook your own vegetables. Not only do you clean your room, you clean an entire house. You even take out the trash without being threatened by your father!

Likewise, there will be times you will have to hug a person, say congratulations, and buy a gift even though you may not feel like it. But when we fail to do the right thing at the right moment, we tend to regret it later. Eventually your feelings will change and you will be glad you committed to a positive action instead of a negative feeling. Just like eating vegetables and cleaning your room, you will realize celebrating was the best thing to do.

Remember, withdrawing during times of celebration communicates volumes. Although we may withhold contemptuous comments and outward expressions of displeasure, our silence can be just as hurtful. Your friend or family member may wonder why you haven't taken time to celebrate with them. While the world is throwing them a party, they can't help but wonder why you decided not to come. Your absence may hurt them and even be misinterpreted. Rise above any selfishness when it's time to celebrate others.

Here are some things to keep in mind if we are to celebrate others in a healthy way.

1. Celebrating requires engagement. Your tendency may be to cut off friends who get in a relationship before you. Disappointment and unpleasant emotions cause you to distance yourself from the reminder of what you do not have. Unfortunately, celebrating is not about a single event or simply saying, "Congratulations." Celebration requires extended engagement. It's calling the person to see how things are going. It's being a cheerleader. It's giving selfless wise counsel. It's taking time out of your busy schedule to spend time with your friend and their significant other. Celebrating is an opportunity for you to be there for others in the same way you would want them to be there for you.

Because of the way humans are wired, we make judgments based on what we see. The best way to let someone know you are celebrating with him or her is by an outward action. This may mean verbalizing it. It may mean showing up at the wedding with a gift. It may mean sending them a congratulations card. It may mean simply being there as a friend.

2. *Celebration requires honesty.* Sometimes, it's healthy to be honest about where you are emotionally. It's natural to feel lonely and left out, and part of the process is being able to be honest with God, yourself, and others. Scripture tells us to have fellowship with other believers and God intends for us to encourage one another. At times, we may have to share our struggles with friends who are enjoying relationships. It's best that they hear the truth from you rather than draw their own conclusions based on the behavior changes they observe. For instance, a friend may read your distant behavior as jealousy although you are just working through your own sadness. It's best to be honest and say, "It is difficult for me to see others dating, but I still love and support you as a friend. I'm extremely happy for you, but I am a little disappointed that I'm not married yet. Please pray for me. I don't want my feelings to strain our friendship. I'm still here for you."

3. *Celebration requires prayer.* One of the greatest ways you can support someone is through prayer. You can accomplish more on your knees than you can anywhere else. You can ask God to bless someone who's in a relationship. You can pray that God grant them wisdom and direction. You can pray as Paul prayed for the saints at Ephesus, that they would comprehend the height and depth of God's love. You can pray that God blesses their relationship and that they don't succumb to temptation. You can pray that the enemy doesn't use past problems to create havoc and division in their relationship. There are many things you can take before the throne of God, and it's difficult to remain bitter and angry with someone you are praying for. Additionally, we

should cast our own cares upon the Lord. You can pray that God will guard your heart against bitterness and jealousy. Our heart tends to follow our prayers.

4. *Celebration requires patience.* If there's any virtue that is essential in the single life, it's patience. Patience is not merely a passive endeavor. It is most evident by your outward behavior while you wait. Isaiah 40:31 is a popular verse: "Yet those who wait for the Lord will gain new strength; they will mount up with wings like eagles, they will run and not get tired, they will walk and not become weary." For many, it's difficult to wrap their heads around the meaning of the verse. "How can waiting on the Lord allow me to gain new strength? Waiting makes me feel weak!"

The context of verse 28 and 29 helps to shed greater light.

"Do you not know? Have you not heard? The Everlasting God, the Lord, the Creator of the ends of the earth does not become weary or tired. His understanding is inscrutable. He gives strength to the weary, and to him who lacks might He increases power."

We serve a God who possesses infinite power and limitless strength. His supply never runs out. We grow weary and tired. We stumble badly. Yet God is able to give strength to those who are weary. When we lack power, God is able to give an increase. We access that limitless supply by simply seeking God and waiting on Him. It is in the process of waiting that God renews and restores us.

5. *Celebration is an investment.* Celebration is an investment in the lives of others and in yourself. Scripture teaches that we reap what we sow. If we sow hatred, we reap hatred. If we sow division, we reap division. If we sow love, we reap love. If we sow

celebration, we will reap celebration. Jesus said that we ought to treat others the way we would like to be treated. This has been said so often it can come across as a cliché, but let it soak in for a minute: as a follower of Christ, I should treat others the same way I wish to one day be treated. If I desire for others to celebrate me, I must first celebrate others.

THE SIN OF COMPARISON

One of the biggest things that will diminish our joy and prevent us from celebrating is making comparisons. Have you ever felt fortunate until you began comparing your life to what someone else possessed? We are content with our parking space until someone gets one closer to the entrance. We are satisfied with a bargain until we discover someone received an even greater deal.

The same is true of romantic relationships. We compare our experiences with others and allow the relationships of others to be the barometer for our happiness. We are content in our singleness until we compare our circumstances with the joy experienced by friends and their mates.

Comparisons can make us frustrated when others get what we want. We may begin to feel more comfortable with individuals who aren't in relationships and alienate people who appear content with their lives. We have pity parties with friends who are also envious and share our same frustrations.

Comparison can also cause pride. We can esteem relationships so highly that we become arrogant when we're in one. Whereas we used to feel left out, we begin to feel as if we are part of a romantic elite.

The comparison game doesn't end with a relationship or a marriage. If you have fallen into the trap of comparing your life with others, you will also compare your spouse, children and quality of living with other families. In life, there will always be someone with bigger and faster and better. You will frown at those with bigger and look down at those with smaller. Comparisons inevitably produce either discontentment or pride.

Ecclesiastes 1:8 says, "The eye is not satisfied with seeing, nor is the ear filled with hearing." Proverbs 27:20 also says, "Sheol and Abaddon are never satisfied, nor are the eyes of man ever satisfied." Our desires are like bottomless pits; the more we get, the more we want. Our appetites are like the ocean; no matter how much water the river dumps in, the ocean never signals "enough." Not only is there no ultimate satisfaction to receiving the things we want, but we never grow satisfied of seeing others fail. There will never be enough broken relationships and divorces to give you a sense of satisfaction. Likewise, no person will bring lasting contentment. We must allow God to plug the hole in our heart.

OUR VIEW OF GOD

The Wilderness of Spectating can distort our view of God. Remember, God's timing in His outpouring of specific blessings is not a reflection of His love for you. Just because others are enjoying God's "blessing" doesn't mean God has forgotten about you. What God does for others has absolutely nothing to do with you and His unconditional love for you. If you measure God's love based on what He gives to others, you will always feel like you received the short end of the stick. God has a specific plan for all and blessings tailor-made for each of us.

Singleness and relationship hurdles are not always signs of God's displeasure. Not being in a relationship is not a curse. Perhaps a relationship ending is the best thing for you right now. God sees things we're unable to see and knows things about our present and future that we're unable to discern. Don't assume God is withholding marriage to punish you for past mistakes and current shortcomings. You can do nothing to "earn" a romantic relationship and we should not serve God as a means to a relational end. Remember, God sees our heart and knows our motives. Serve God because He is worthy to be worshiped and honored.

You must also be careful not to impose misguided expectations upon God. Do not assume that an instance of obedience will yield the outcome you desire or that celebrating others is a shortcut to your dream. I've heard people rejoice with others and then say, "I know my blessing is coming," all in the same breath. This creates an expectation of God that He may not choose to meet. We should never give in order to get. Celebrate others because it's the right thing to do.

THE CELEBRATION QUADRANTS

There are four quadrants we may find ourselves in when celebrating others.

SAD FOR YOU HAPPY FOR ME Q3	HAPPY FOR YOU HAPPY FOR ME Q4
SAD FOR YOU SAD FOR ME Q2	HAPPY FOR YOU SAD FOR ME Q1

Quadrant 1 is most common. It's when we are happy for another person, but saddened that we aren't experiencing the same good things. We attend the engagement party and wedding and even dance at the reception. Inwardly, however, we can't help but be sad because we are not in a relationship or the one we have is not working out. Lingering in Quadrant 1 leads to jealousy and resentment. Consequently, we inevitably end up in Quadrant 2.

Quadrant 2 is when we are unhappy with both our situation and those of others. Not only are you upset that you aren't seeing anyone, but you are unhappy when you learn others are in a relationship. Murmuring and complaining characterize Quadrant 2. We are probably most depressed in this quadrant, which can be emotionally and spiritually draining. The danger in this quadrant is we may abandon hope and become ungrateful. We may fail to recognize God's goodness and can ignore the blessings He has already bestowed.

Quadrant 3 is when we are happy for us, but sad for the other person. At first glance this may not fully make sense. How is it that we can be happy with our own lives and feel sorrow toward others who are in a happy place? The key to understanding this quadrant is recognizing the presence of masked discontentment in our lives. Our sadness towards others is a defense mechanism for the hurt we are truly feeling or the disappointment we secretly feel in our own relationship. We may feel or talk negatively about relationships, marriage, and persons of the opposite sex. Those in a healthy relationship or who share chemistry are looked upon with suspicion. Meanwhile, we pretend as if everything is going great in our lives. It may be difficult for us to recognize when we're in Quadrant 3 because this is often when we deceive ourselves most.

Quadrant 4 is where we ideally need to be. This is where we are genuinely happy for others as well as for ourselves. We learn how to celebrate others without turning it into a pity party for ourselves. This is the quadrant where we experience true contentment, abandoning the scarcity mentality and recognizing there is no need to compete for a relationship. We realize our future is not threatened by others' fortune. We serve a God who provides out of His abundant supply. We may be limited, but we serve a limitless God. The key to staying in this quadrant is contentment and a healthy regard for God's sovereignty. The foundation is a rock-solid belief that God is causing all things to work together for good.

Remaining in Quadrant 4 requires strength and perseverance. You will find yourself drifting into the other quadrants. Don't give up.

ANOTHER'S POSSESSION

While you're in The Wilderness of Spectating, you may have to grapple with the idea of "possession." God mentions that the land was given to the sons of Lot as a possession. One of the most difficult things is to be a spectator as your ex or someone you admire from afar connects with another person. It can feel like a stab in the back. You may feel a sense of entitlement or "ownership" of a person as you see individuals with whom you were formerly involved move on to other relationships. Some may even marry before you do. But just because you dated or knew someone before his spouse or her current relationship doesn't give you the right of possession. You may especially tend to feel this way if there wasn't a sense of closure in the relationship. Some relationships tend to end with a question mark rather than a period, leaving us to wonder if things have truly ended. Once a relationship is over, it's over. Some people remain emotionally connected with people who have moved on. But when a relationship ends, we must relinquish all rights and privileges.

Sometimes, you may not still have feelings for the other person but watching them move toward the altar faster than you is still a challenge. You may have feelings of regret. You may see them grow in areas that contributed to your breakup. You may ask yourself, "Did I make a mistake ending the relationship? Did I end it too soon? Should I have hung in there a little bit longer?" This can even happen after a marriage ends; when the other person remarries, starts another family, and experiences a successful marriage the first spouse can feel dejected from the sidelines.

Regardless of the circumstances, our job is not to play God and try to figure out His plan. We are not the Holy Spirit. In The Wilderness of Spectating, we are called to celebrate. You'll be glad you did.

VICTORIA'S STORY

Victoria is no stranger to The Wilderness of Spectating. As a single woman in her thirties, she has witnessed many of her friends experience romantic relationships and get married. Meanwhile, Victoria has experienced unsuccessful dating relationships. Her desire to find someone with whom she is spiritually compatible has been challenging. Her desire to please God and not compromise her values has resulted in being alone many times. Relationships in which she did share the same values seemed to have ended due to God's sovereignty.

Despite not being in a relationship, Victoria has continuously championed her friends who have been. In college, she met three people who made a significant impact on her life. Throughout her years in undergrad, they bonded as they prayed together, supported each other, and studied God's Word together. A few years after graduating, one of those friends entered into a relationship. As it developed, Victoria remained genuinely happy and supportive. When her friend was preparing to marry, she asked Victoria to be in the wedding and Victoria accepted the invitation without hesitation. Her two other college friends later became engaged and married to each other. Once again, Victoria was asked to be in their wedding and she accepted the invitation and celebrated with them.

But there was more—over the span of four years, Victoria was part of at least one wedding per year. She even flew across the United States to surprise one of her friends for a bridal shower. Victoria played an active part in each wedding, assisting with planning, set-up for events, and anything her friends asked. While Victoria tends to have a strong, outgoing personality, she always made sure the attention was on the bride.

However, Victoria has had her weak moments. As she's celebrated her friends, she's had feelings of sadness and envy. It was difficult at times to witness romantic moments. Sometimes, she would look around the room only to notice that she was the only single person. But she realized she couldn't allow her identity to be defined by that one moment or by her relationship status.

Through God's grace, she has been able to stay "Happy for Them and Happy for Her." Instead of waiting around for a husband, she is determined to maximize the time God has given her. She has pursued her passions, gone on mission trips at a moment's notice, started graduate school, and taken advantage of opportunities to travel to new places. She knows things will change if she gets married, and she's determined to take advantage of the flexibility she has a single person. She realizes that the secret to being the biggest cheerleader is being content. Victoria says, "I'm committed to live in the moment. Once a moment is gone, you cannot get it back."

LANDMARKS

- The Wilderness of Spectating is where I watch God provide for everyone except me.
- In The Wilderness of Spectating, I must celebrate others.
- My goal is to remain Happy for You and Happy for Me.
- The blessings God bestows on others are not a reflection of His love for me.

CHAPTER SIX

THE LAND OF LOVE

> *Arise, set out, and pass through the valley of Arnon. Look! I have given Sihon the Amorite, king of Heshbon, and his land into your hand; begin to take possession and contend with him in battle. This day I will begin to put the dread and fear of you upon the peoples everywhere under the heavens, who, when they hear the report of you, will tremble and be in anguish because of you.*
>
> Deuteronomy 2:24-25

For the first time on their journey, Israel is promised to gain the victory and possess land. Here is the moment! After almost forty years of journeying in the wilderness, they will finally have a land to call their own. They would go on to possess the entire kingdom of Sihon and all its cities. According to Numbers 22:25, they would take control of land from the Arnon to the Jabbok. They would possess all of Hebron and its villages. The territory they would possess extended from Aroer and half of Gilead.

The last stage is called The Land of Love. The Land of Love

is when you finally meet someone you want to be with and take that relationship into the realm of marriage. You finally "possess land." After years of wandering back and forth between The Mountain of Acceptance, Plateau of Comfort, Wilderness of Spectating, and Valley of One, you finally enter The Land of Love. You look into that person's eyes and say, "I do."

It's the land that most people dream about. In fact, you may have been so anxious you skipped over the other chapters and jumped right to this one. (If you have, go back and read the other chapters first. You'll be glad you did!)

PREPARE FOR BATTLE

God told Israel they would possess the land, but not without a fight. You're probably thinking, "Fight? What do you mean fight? Are you serious?" Yes—a commitment to possess The Land of Love is a commitment to fight. The Land of Love is also the land of conflict. When people think of love, they think of "settling down" and living happily ever after. But many people who get to The Land of Love aren't happy.

About 50% of first-time marriages end in divorce. In addition, 67% of second marriages and 74% of third marriages end in divorce. It seems the more opportunities someone has to enter the land, the more prone the marriage is to failure. The church is not far behind; approximately 42% of Christian marriages end in divorce.

The problem usually isn't that the two people aren't in love. The problem is they don't know how to fight when disagreements inevitably come. They are great at romance, but terrible at handling conflicts. Eventually, conflicts destroy the romance.

As a result, The Land of Love is not always a place of joy.

Some couples find themselves living a life of frustration, anger, depression, sorrow and regret. Some even feel deceived. Some wish they were in The Land of Love with someone else. Most married individuals contemplate divorce at some point in the marriage.

A LAND OF CONFLICT

At this point, I need to redefine The Land of Love. The Land of Love is where you enlist in a life-long commitment to fight for your marriage. The question is not whether you will have conflict, it's just a question of when. The key to keeping a marriage alive is for both people to know how to fight.

There are three types of conflict married people must conquer to be victorious in The Land of Love. Believe it or not, these battles tend to be ongoing. One of the reasons for divorce in the United States is "irreconcilable differences." This usually means the couple was unable to resolve this ongoing conflict.

1. Internal conflict. People bring baggage into a marriage, including personal internal struggles. We wrestle with the flesh. Inside of us there's a tug of war between righteousness and unrighteousness; good and evil; sin and sanctification. If you have been walking with God for any amount of time, you already know this is a non-stop battle. Part of you wants to be honest and another part wants to live a lie. Part of you wants to be kind and the other part wants to be angry and fierce. Part of you wants to please your spouse and the other part wants to please yourself. Part of you wants to spend time with your children and the other part is tempted to forsake them for things that seem more urgent. Part of you wants to be sexually pure and the other part lusts and craves impurity. The list goes on and on.

We also wrestle with insecurities and self-worth, wondering if we are good husbands, wives, fathers, and citizens. We often compare ourselves to others or to what society portrays as the ideal, and when we haven't achieved certain material possessions or status, we question our self-worth. This type of internal conflict can cause conflict and create tension in a marriage.

2. *Interpersonal Conflict.* Marriage is a perfect covenant between two imperfect people. Everyone brings imperfection into the marriage. No one magically becomes perfect when he gets married. As a matter of fact, marriage can sometime heighten and expose our imperfections even more. You'll be surprised to discover imperfections you didn't even realized you had!

For some couples, conflict begins during the honeymoon. Someone forgets to wash the dishes. Someone neglects to take out the trash. Someone raises their voice and becomes defensive during a conversation. Someone doesn't keep a promise.

These are normal, everyday things that can cause turmoil. Marital conflict is like lifting your arms parallel to the ground. At first, it's pretty bearable. Not a big deal. But after a while, your arms start to become tired. Suddenly, it's not fun anymore. What you thought was just a minor issue becomes an unbearable burden.

However, the conflicts themselves are not necessarily the source of marital problems. Problems usually arise with how we address the conflict. Two couples can experience exactly the same conflict. For one couple, the conflict draws them closer together. For the other couple, it drives them further apart. Healthy conflict resolution makes the difference.

Ephesians 4:26-27 says, "Be angry, and yet do not sin; do not let the sun go down on your anger, and do not give the devil an opportunity." Anger is a natural emotion. Will your spouse do things in marriage to make you angry? Yes! Will there be things in life that frustrate and disappoint you? Absolutely! Getting angry is not necessarily sinful in and of itself. It's how we deal with the anger.

Notice, the passage doesn't say, "Do not be angry." It says, "In your anger do not sin." How can a person sin through anger? This passage says we sin when we "allow the sun to go down" on our anger—when we allow our hurt, disappointment, and frustration to remain unaddressed. Suppressing our anger and hurt gives the devil an opportunity to steal, kill, and destroy. He wants to tear families apart, and one of the ways he gains a foothold is through unresolved conflict.

Couples should fight the problem, not each other. Your wife or your husband is not the problem. The problem is the problem. We wrestle not against flesh and blood, but against spiritual wickedness in high places. Behind almost every conflict, Satan is hiding in the shadows. Victorious couples are able to see beyond each other and address the problem from a spiritual perspective. Instead of letting a problem remain unresolved, they talk about it in a healthy, constructive way. They pray together. They take their burdens before the Lord. As one spouse addresses his anger and frustration, the other person listens. If there was a violation, the guilty party asks for forgiveness and the offended one forgives.

3. External Conflicts. Even when a couple does not find themselves in conflict with each other, they may be at odds with a third party. Perhaps it is family members who are against your marriage. Some family members may not like one of the individuals in the marriage or one spouse may not get along with the in-laws. A couple may find themselves at odds with a church or a spiritual leader. One of the individuals may have a child from a previous marriage or relationship that may be a source of tension or there may also be conflicts with an ex-spouse. One of the spouses may work for an organization that demands a lot of time and energy. A couple may find themselves having to go to court with a person or organization. A couple may find themselves in conflict with the difficulties of life: health problems, tragedies, automobile accidents, natural disasters, and unforeseen circumstances.

Any of these external conflicts can put a strain on a marriage. The couple may disagree about how to handle the conflict, and if they are not careful the tension of the battle can pull them further apart. Sometimes, one of the individuals may feel pressured to choose between her spouse or another person or pursuit. Of course, this seems like a no-brainer–choose your spouse! Yet for many, their love for a family member or their drive to pursue a dream can make them feel as if their spouse is a hindrance or obstacle. Some other people in your life, such as parents, siblings, children, and close friends, may even pressure you into choosing them over your spouse. All of these scenarios place real pressure on a marriage.

CHOOSING YOUR BATTLES WISELY

I know you may be head-over-heels in love. You may even be convinced you have met the person God wants you to be with. Here is the big question you must ask yourself: is this a battle I am willing to fight? There are some conflicts and people that may not be worth the fight. A person who refuses to prioritize you over their dreams, friends, and family may already be demonstrating that your future marriage will be no contest for external conflict. A person who experiences major internal conflict, yet refuses to get help or trust in the Lord, may demonstrate they are not ready to take on the additional pressures of marriage. The Israelite battle with King Sihon was not a worthless fight. It had kingdom purposes because it was the beginning of a series of battles that would lead to them finally possessing the Promised Land. Not every battle is worth enlisting for.

The conflict and problems will only intensify after marriage. Whatever you see now, just go ahead and multiply it by ten. If he's abusing you now, he'll abuse you ten times more in marriage. If she's selfish now, she'll be ten times more selfish in marriage. If his children despise you now, they'll despise you more after you are married. The goal here is not to paint a bleak, hopeless picture that God is unable to resolve. However, there are times God reveals red flags to us. Don't ignore them. Address them. If they can't be addressed, you may have a hard choice to make.

THE VALUE OF CONFLICT

King Sihon refused to let the Israelites enter the land because God hardened his heart. It's almost as if God is the boxing manager that put the fight together. God uses conflicts to strengthen us and accomplish His will. For the Israelites, He used the conflict to create an opportunity to seize the land.

Conflicts are also opportunities for God to accomplish His will in a marriage. Conflicts teach us how to better trust God and they enable two people to learn more about each other and how to better treat one another. They allow us to grow in wisdom, patience, love, understanding, and kindness. They deepen our prayer life. James 1:1-4 talks about enduring through trials.

God wants the trial to have its perfect work in us, strengthening both individuals and the marriage.

This requires initiative on our part. It means choosing not to bail out of something because it's hard. It's resisting the urge to quit and walk away. It's refusing to look for the easy way out. It's submitting to the sovereign work of God. Some conflicts are short, while others can be quite lengthy. Some conflicts may take a series of conversations over an extended period of time. But you must let them "have their perfect way."

God desires for every marriage to be victorious, but victory only comes with a fight. Victory only comes after two people have a chance to duke it out against a problem. Healing comes after the counseling sessions. Forgiveness comes after confession. Restoration comes after forgiveness. Reconciliation comes after humility. Gain comes after sacrifice. Problems are resolved after the hard conversations. Victory comes after the battle.

Very often, God told Israel to utterly destroy a city. This was the case in Deuteronomy 2. Verse 34 tells us they left no survivor. Similarly, a couple should seek to utterly destroy the issues they face. We should eliminate selfishness, or materialism, or infidelity and immorality. When addressing an issue, the aim should be to deal with it thoroughly.

Many couples are like Saul in 1 Samuel 15. Samuel instructed Saul to utterly destroy the Amalekites. However, he chose not to and blamed it on his soldiers. Like Saul, we seek to address the problem but don't utterly destroy the spoil. While seeking to reconcile over infidelity, one of the individuals has someone they are still "kind of seeing." A couple talks about financial difficulties, but never commit to saving, giving, and establishing a budget. Someone asks for forgiveness, but the other person continues to harbor bitterness even after saying, "I forgive you."

Another way we fail to utterly destroy is by beginning to address an issue but not following through. For example, someone may stop going to counseling after a few sessions. A couple may begin attending a small group at their church, but begin tapering off. They start fighting, but walk off the field in the middle of the battle.

Perhaps you're saying, "I'm not married, so I don't really need to hear about this conflict resolution stuff." Not so fast! There are several things you must realize as a single person:

1. We take our conflict resolution style into marriage. In the dating and courting phase, it's easy to put your best foot forward. You can be so infatuated with love that you and your partner brush over conflicts. One look into each other's eyes and you say, "What conflict? The only conflict I have is my love for you." (By the way, I did come up with that cheesy line all by myself.)

But once two people say I do, reality kicks in. Once the passion and honeymoon phase dies off, it's business as usual. You will deal with conflict with your spouse like you do in your other relationships.

Some people's tendency is to go into fight mode and attack. Whenever they are offended or confronted, they yell or throw objects or slam doors or attack the other person with their words. They might even attack physically.

Others deal with conflict by going into flight mode. Instead of attacking, they retreat, leaving the room or giving the silent treatment. They tend to suppress their true feelings. When asked if they are doing OK, they tend to say, "I'm fine," but their tone of voice indicates the opposite. Another way some people go into flight mode is by trying to change the subject during a conversation. Whatever tactic they choose, retreating never resolves conflict; it just suppresses it and leads to a greater explosion at a later time.

2. *Many couples tend to face unsuspected conflict on their way to the altar.* When two people decide to be with one another, everyone may be happy and excited. However, there's an enemy who is not thrilled about the marriage. He's not excited about the potential two people may have to bring God glory and advance His kingdom. Therefore he will throw fiery darts in hopes of causing discouragement, division, and disillusionment.

On the other hand, we have a God who allows us to go through obstacles as a test. He hopes we will come out of the refiner's fire as pure gold. Sometimes, we come out of the fire as charred wood, but that's because we need to mature.

Here are some conflicts that people encounter on their way to the altar:

- A constant tug of war with future in-laws.
- Parents, family members, and friends beginning to feel threatened by your significant other. They feel that you loving your partner means less time and love for them. They may express it in ways that are hurtful and discouraging.
- Your friends, some of whom you love dearly, begin to become envious of your relationship.
- Wedding plans become frustrating and overly challenging.
- The couple argues on the wedding day.
- Family members who disapprove of your spouse decide to boycott the wedding.
- You have to remove individuals from the wedding party

due to lack of cooperation and other difficulties.
- One or both parents refuses to give their blessing of the union.
- There are logistical challenges such as the marriage license or the tuxedos not being ready.
- The couple's personalities and values clash.
- Suspicious individuals plant seeds of discord and slander.
- The couple experiences difficulty finding and maintaining employment.
- You find out your partner has been keeping secrets from you.

3. Your current challenges may be preparation ground for future conflict. God has a way of using now to prepare us for then. Conflicts tend to seem like a useless inconvenience. Who looks forward to butting heads with a boyfriend? Who wants to face moments of tension with family members? Yet God may be using these moments to refine us. God may not necessarily be the one causing the conflict, but He allows it. God has a way of working all things together for the good of those who love Him and are called according to His purpose.

KEEPING IT HEALTHY

One of the greatest ways to prepare for The Land of Love is to learn to resolve conflicts in a healthy way that deepens a relationship rather than damages it. What's the sense of resolving a conflict if it will only hurt the person and destroy the relationship? Here are some steps you can take to resolve conflicts in a healthy manner.

1. Seek out the person who has hurt you for a conversation. The goal is to resolve conflicts as soon as possible. Remember that

Ephesians 4:26 says, "Do not let the sun go down on your anger." Does this mean you have to sit at a window looking to see when the sun will set as your deadline? Probably not. Does this mean that we should pray Joshua's prayer that the sun stands still? I don't think that's the point Paul was trying to make.

Rather, the idea is to seek reconciliation as soon as possible. If someone has hurt or offended you, you should go to that person. Don't wait for him to come to you. You may say, "Well, she started it!" "It was his fault." Though that may be true, you are the one carrying the emotional weight. There will not be any sense of peace in your heart until you make the first step to resolve the issue. Simply ask the person if you can talk to her about an issue that's on your heart. You may agree on a future time and place if that moment is not the best.

Some people come right out and try to address the issue. "I can't believe you didn't show up last night!" "You made me so angry!" Whenever you approach situations like this, it comes across as an attack. The other person than becomes defensive and may go into fight or flight mode. Setting an appointment can give both individuals an opportunity to pray and gather their thoughts. You are also able to have better control of the direction and mood of the conversation.

2. Be honest about your feelings. You must be honest about the hurt, frustration, or anger the situation caused you. In Ephesians 4:25 Paul said we are to lay aside falsehood and speak the truth to one another. Conflicts are only resolved when the truth is addressed. Again, you don't want to attack the person. Instead, focus on your feelings. Share why you felt embarrassed when the person made an inappropriate joke or how unsafe you felt when the person placed you in a compromising position. Zero in on how unimportant you felt when you were not recognized for a contribution you made. When you focus on how you feel, it doesn't come across as an attack on what the other person may or may not have done. Of course, this is not to say that you ignore the actions of the other person. It will still come up in the conversation. But focus the conversation on how you felt and thought about the situation.

3. Have a humble and forgiving heart. If the other person is at fault, hopefully he will see his mistake, own up to it, and apologize. If you were the one who was wrong, you should be willing to apologize. Conflict resolution comes to a halt when there's more of a desire to justify bad behavior than to pursue reconciliation. However, this is different from offering an apology with explanation. An apology with explanation is not giving excuses, but rather offering context so the action is better understood. As the person who feels offended, it is only fair to listen to the explanation and try to better understand the problem.

Once a person has asked to be forgiven, it is up to the other person. In Matthew 6:14-15, Jesus said, "For if you forgive others for their transgressions, your heavenly Father will also forgive you. But if you do not forgive others, then your Father will not forgive your transgressions."

Remember, forgiveness is a gift. It's not something you can earn. Jesus never asks us to earn His forgiveness, but forgives us of our transgressions freely. Sometimes, it may take time to regain trust in a person. However, trusting and forgiveness are two different things. You can forgive a person as she seeks to regain your trust.

4. Establish a plan. Once forgiveness has been sought and given, the question is, "Then what?" Sometimes, two people can be so happy for there to be forgiveness that they forget to develop a plan for moving forward differently. Without a plan, they simply end up back in the same situation several months, weeks, or even days later!

A plan simply means stating what has to change so the action isn't repeated. For example, a plan might be that I will call whenever I am running late, or I will be more sensitive about comments I make about you in a public setting. A plan says I will be more careful to write things down so I don't forget or I will do everything in my power to not respond in anger.

Having a plan allows there to be accountability. Both individuals should participate in coming up with this agreement and both people can then remember it as the basis for future actions. Proverbs 16:1 says plans come from the heart of man, and Proverbs 16:3 says man is then to commit his works to the Lord, so that his plans may be established. Remember, failing to plan is planning to fail.

SHAWN AND THERESA'S STORY

Shawn and Theresa have been married for about three years. They met as children because their parents were friends. Shawn's family lived out of the country and would visit the United States each summer. When Theresa was in college they began dating seriously for two years even though they only saw each other during summer vacations.

The distance began placing a strain on the relationship. In addition, Theresa began growing in her walk with God but Shawn was not very committed to Christ. Their relationship eventually ended and they didn't see each other for five years. During that time, Shawn recommitted his life to Jesus Christ, which opened the door for them to reunite and rekindle their relationship. After courting for two more years, Shawn and Theresa married.

However, they discovered The Land of Love was a place of conflict. During their courting phase, they faced conflict with their families. Theresa's mother expressed her concerns about Shawn and the relationship. She felt that Shawn and Theresa were not prepared for marriage and should be more financially established. She also wanted to see them complete their educational pursuits. In addition, Shawn had recently moved to the United States and was still transitioning, while Theresa still carried some emotional baggage from a previous relationship. She had to make some tough decisions to help her move on from her past and begin building a healthy future with Shawn.

Despite these concerns, Shawn and Theresa decided to get married. The first year of their marriage was difficult. External and internal conflicts began taking a toll on their marriage. Even though Theresa's mother did not interfere, the residue of her pre-marital concerns trickled into their marriage. At times, Shawn felt Theresa was taking her mother's side. When Theresa would try to explain why her mother may have felt a certain way, Shawn interpreted it as Theresa defending her mother.

In addition, Theresa sometimes felt Shawn was not opening up to her emotionally and was not compassionate when she was hurting. They had difficulties communicating and understanding each other. Shawn often needed time to think about issues before responding while Theresa felt the need to respond immediately by saying whatever was on her mind. As much as they knew they had to rely on God, they didn't always resolve issues with prayer and had some very heated arguments. Not only did they "let the sun go down" on their anger, they once went to bed so angry they slept with their backs turned to each other.

Shawn and Theresa realized something had to be done if their new marriage was going to survive. They decided to see a marriage counselor. They began to understand each other's communication styles. They learned to be open and compassionate towards one another. Shawn began building a better relationship with Theresa's mother and as Theresa's mother became more accepting of Shawn, they were able to iron out their miscommunications and disagreements. They also learned the importance of establishing healthy boundaries, including what issues they would keep private and what they would share with their families. They learned to filter outside voices and influences and began prioritizing each other more.

They also remained committed to keeping Jesus Christ at the center of their marriage. They prayed together, spent time together, and had family devotions. They've worked together to help other married friends who also have marriage difficulties. What could have ended Shawn and Theresa's marriage was used to draw them closer together, and today they remain committed to fighting for their marriage.

LANDMARKS

- The Land of Love is where I enlist in a life-long commitment to fight for my marriage.
- In The Land of Love, I will have to face internal, interpersonal, and external conflict.
- Before I get married, I must ask if this is a battle worth fighting.
- How I resolve conflicts when I'm single determines how I resolve conflicts when I'm married.

- I can prepare for The Land of Love by learning to resolve conflicts in a healthy manner.
- I must resolve conflicts in a way that deepens rather than damages relationships.

CHAPTER SEVEN
OUR STORY

For the last chapter, I thought it would be a great idea for me and my wife to share our personal experiences in each relationship terrain. We hope you can learn from our experiences!

JUMAINE'S EXPERIENCE

Mountain of Acceptance
As a young Christian single, I was absent from the dating scene. It was never my desire to date multiple women or drift from one woman to the next. Before approaching a young lady, I always wanted to feel a sense of God leading or nudging me. Not all of my friends shared the same perspective. Some of them felt I should be more proactive and intentional about meeting more women. A friend once told me, "Jumaine, you spend such a long time praying about it that by the time you've prayed about it, the lady's gone."

Also, from the time I rededicated my life to Christ, I was always in some sort of leadership position, from a junior high Sunday school teacher or youth ministry worker to church ministry intern or, eventually, associate pastor. I never wanted my "good to be evil spoken of." I never wanted to develop a reputation of breaking women's hearts or give anyone a reason to question my integrity with women.

During seminary I first began expressing interest in women as a dedicated Christian. Throughout college, I pretty much stayed away from dating and focused on my spiritual development. Now, it was time for me to come out of my shell. However, most of the women I was interested in did not show much interest in me. For instance, there was one young lady with whom I developed a great rapport. After spending significant time together and speaking on the phone, I felt it was time to discuss where our relationship was headed. I shared that I really liked her and was curious if she felt the same way about me. She responded by stating she needed time to think about it. After a few days of pondering, she let me know she did not feel the same way but wanted us to remain friends. I also recall my interactions with another young lady. I always enjoyed talking with her and our conversations were almost always centered on scripture and the things of God. But before I got a chance to express my feelings to her, she told me she was beginning to develop feelings for me, but knew it was not time for her to be in a relationship.

Unlike many who have been on The Mountain of Acceptance, I did not experience a long-term relationship. However, I did struggle when discovering that someone I liked was not the person God had for me. My trips down the mountain were difficult at times. I questioned my manhood. I allowed rejection to be the barometer of my self-worth. I wondered if I was handsome enough or if I needed a more muscular physique. During a meeting with my pastor, I burst into tears. I couldn't understand why I couldn't find the right type of woman and I wondered what in the world was wrong with me.

But despite the difficult moments, I remained able to embrace God's sovereignty. Even though I didn't always understand my circumstances, I knew that God loved me and knew what was best for me.

Plateau of Comfort
After several failed attempts to meet a godly woman, I started wondering if my standards were a bit too high. I thought, "Maybe it's unrealistic to expect women to know as much about scripture as I do. Being in seminary may have caused me to lose touch with the 'normal, everyday' Christian woman." Approximately one year after graduating from seminary, I met a young lady. Unlike other women in the past, she wanted to be in a relationship with me. She showered me with love and attention and we spent time hanging out and getting to know each other better.

As things progressed I began to see red flags. However, I found comfort in knowing someone loved me for who I was. Finally, someone thought I was handsome. I didn't have to look like one of the guys from the cover of a magazine. Finally, I was good enough. But as I sought God about the situation, I felt Him say, "This is not who I have for you." I finally had to be honest with her about the direction of our relationship. I shared my concerns with her, how I felt God was leading me, and that we needed to remain friends. She was heartbroken and disappointed and so was I. I realized having to reject someone was just as difficult as being rejected.

About one year later, I found myself back on The Plateau of Comfort. I had been friends with a young woman for several years. She was attractive, godly, and pleasant. Like the previous relationship, I was flattered that she was attracted to me and accepted me just as I was. One evening, we both shared our feelings for one another.

There was one problem, however. She was still in a serious relationship with someone else. She said she wasn't convinced he was the right person for her. What I should have viewed as a huge red flag, I instead welcomed as a challenge. I was determined to show her what being with a true man of God looked like. Once she received clarity from God, she would surely see that the other guy wasn't God's best for her.

This was not the way things panned out. We continued to talk, but her relationship with the other guy never ended. The more I developed feelings for her, the easier it seemed to ignore her relationship with him. I knew this was not a healthy way to build a relationship that would lead to marriage. One day, she finally admitted that she felt he was the person God had for her. I was disappointed, but I encouraged her to hold fast to what God had shown her.

My Plateau of Comfort relationships taught me to approach future relationships with more humility, discernment, and wisdom.

Valley of One
Even though I had my fair share of romantic interests, most of my single years were spent alone. Not being in many relationships afforded me time to focus on God. I decided early in my Christian walk to maximize my singleness. Many of my friends were consumed with wanting to be in a relationship, but I didn't want my life to be focused on trying to find a mate. I wanted it

to be marked with contentment and influence, not discontentment and murmuring.

After graduating from college, I decided to attend seminary in Texas. I had never been there before and it was a complete step of faith. I remember taking a taxi from the airport having no idea when the vehicle would stop! I soon began working in the inner city of south Dallas and had the opportunity to impact the lives of children, teenagers, and families. God used me as a spiritual example to others and even used me to lead people to a saving knowledge of Jesus.

I also spent time volunteering for the youth ministry at my local church and during my last two years in seminary I became an intern. I also went on my first mission trip during this time, traveling to eight different islands in a span of ten weeks to work on various ministry projects. Being a single person afforded me the flexibility to take advantage of such a great opportunity. After my seminary training, I left Dallas to return to the Washington, D.C. area to be part of a church planting team. I stepped out on faith without the promise of a salary. Unlike many married people that would have to count the cost before making such a big move, I was able to do it on short notice.

The Valley of One was also a place of pruning. God pruned my tendency to "over-spiritualize" relationships. I sometimes read into situations as signs or confirmation from God. This resulted in me giving my heart too soon and declaring a move of God too quickly. I remember seeking the Lord concerning whether a young lady may have been the one. I said, "God, if she is who you have for me, allow me to see a sign today." Later that day, I received a poem via email from another person who previously caught my attention. Within minutes, the other young lady sent me the exact same poem! I was completely blown away! But in spite of "the sign," the relationship didn't go anywhere. In The Valley of One, I learned the difference between waiting for God to speak and assuming God was speaking. I learned that being convinced of a woman was not enough; she also had to be convinced God sent me into her life. The same God that was able to speak to me would also speak to her.

Most importantly, in The Valley of One I grew closer to God. God continuously molded me into the man He was calling me to be. In The Valley of One I learned to be a true worshipper of God and learned honesty and trust. It is where God taught me how to walk by faith.

It was also a time for me to prepare for a future marriage. He gave me wisdom on how to be a godly husband and a good financial steward. I was able to become debt-free and build savings. I learned to resist temptation in The Valley of One. I remember as a young Christian resisting the temptation to be sexually intimate with a young lady. I would never have guessed I would end up introducing her to my wife almost fifteen years later! It felt great being able to do it without any sense of guilt or regret.

I officially left The Valley of One on March 12, 2005 when I married my wife Dafnette. As I prepared to marry her, I reflected on my single life. I was honestly able to say that I maximized my singleness. I was able to bring closure to my single life without regret.

Wilderness of Spectating

Much of my single years were spent as a spectator. As I failed to be successful in the area of romance, people around me were enjoying healthy romantic relationships. I even witnessed the wedding of some of my closest friends. Initially, this didn't bother me—it delighted me to celebrate others. The older I became, however, the more difficult it was to be a spectator. One evening when I was a seminary student, I attended a banquet. After the event, all my friends left with their spouses or significant others. As I waved goodbye to my friends, I realized I was going home alone. For the first time, I felt left out. I thought, "I'm in my late twenties and still single. The clock is ticking!"

One of my greatest challenges was seeing women I was interested in entering into relationships with other guys. One day, I began reflecting on all my past "relationships." My mind filled up with negative thoughts. I thought how naïve and unwise some of the women were. I thought, "What were they thinking? What made them think they were better than me? Don't they know they missed out on an opportunity to be with a strong, godly man?"

God interrupted my thoughts and convicted me of my pride and arrogance. I immediately dropped to my knees and did two things. First, I repented of bitterness. I had no right to think this way about these women, and God was not pleased with my thoughts. Second, I prayed for each of them. I literally prayed, "God, I want you to bless their socks off." I prayed that prayer for them because this is what I desired for me—I wanted God to bless my socks off with a great woman. Throughout the years, I have seen God answer that prayer. One by one, God blessed each and every one of those ladies. They went on to marry godly men and raise beautiful children. By no means do I credit all their blessings to my prayer. Yet, this was a defining moment for me. Regardless of what I felt at the time, I knew I had to begin celebrating them.

Land of Love

I met my beautiful wife Dafnette on Friday, October 11, 2002. Earlier that day, I received an e-mail from an acquaintance inviting me and one of my friends to a bowling outing. To be honest, I almost missed the message. I decided to check my e-mail one last time for the day. I called my friend to see if he was interested in going. I assumed we would decline since the invite came at such short notice, but we both agreed to go.

The first person we met in the bowling alley was Dafnette. Her beauty and godliness stuck out to me. She shined like a bright light that was difficult to ignore.

Several weeks later, I decided to watch a video series I had stored away in a box from my Dallas move. It was a series on the Song of Solomon by Tommy Nelson, pastor of Denton Bible Fellowship in Denton, TX. After viewing the series, I got before God and listed 29 essential things I knew I needed to have in a future mate. As my feelings and interest towards Dafnette grew, I discovered she matched all the attributes on the list. I knew then and there I had found the right woman for me.

By this time, I had grown to be more discerning and learned not to jump to conclusions about a woman's feelings for me. If there was anything I learned from my past relationship pursuits, I knew I had to walk in wisdom and let things unfold in God's timing. A few weeks later I expressed my interest in her. She shared that she felt the same way about me. Over time, I allowed the friendship to build and God continued to affirm that Dafnette was an answer to prayer. Dafnette was the first person with whom I shared a serious, long-term relationship. After a time of dating and courtship, we married on March 12, 2005.

Throughout the years, we've grown together and enjoyed our marriage. However, marriage has not come without challenges. Our personality traits and habits have been a source of interpersonal conflict. For instance, my wife is very organized and tends to be a planner. I, on the other hand, tend to be very disorganized and free-spirited. My disorganization has frustrated her as I've allowed important tasks and responsibilities to fall through the cracks. Likewise, my tendency to procrastinate has often communicated to her that I didn't take her concerns to heart, while I have accused her of being controlling and insensitive. Her honesty in bringing issues to light has made me feel as if she was being overly critical of me. But as we talk through these issues we've found healthy ways to communicate our frustrations and resolve conflict. We've found healthy communication and conflict resolution to play an essential role in the success of our marriage.

During our marriage, we've also realized the importance of establishing and maintaining boundaries. Both of us currently work at our church, The Bridge, and have a heart for ministry. Our passion for ministry can sometime consume us and spill over into our marriage. If we're not careful, our dates and personal time together can turn into ministry planning meetings. It is easy to place more time, energy, and creativity into ministry than our home. Not maintaining healthy boundaries has resulted in some tense and heated moments. As much as we love our church and the people who attend, there are times we must "shut it off" for the sake of our marriage. Despite the ups and downs, I still believe God answered my prayer and "blessed my socks off!"

DAFNETTE'S STORY

Although I'm married today, I vividly remember the challenges of my relationship journey. I wanted to get married since I was young. As an adolescent, I could read an (age-appropriate!) romance novel in less than a day. These filled my head with the possible ways I might meet that special someone and how our relationship might unfold. None of these fantasies came to fruition.

High school marked a significant turning point in my life: I began living for Christ. But my newfound devotion to God did not diminish my romantic fantasies; instead, it refined my standards and made me more intent on being in a relationship with a particular type of male. Not only did I desire a mate who was physically attractive and capable of protecting me, I desired someone who loved God. Clearly, my standards were a work in progress later refined by adult realities and responsibilities. Nevertheless, my desire for a godly man, I believe, made my journey more of a challenge.

Mountain of Acceptance

Because a personal, growing relationship with Christ was a minimum requirement for a potential suitor, it was not difficult for me to decline the advances of certain men. To my disappointment, however, advances by men who seemed godly were few and far between. Thus attention from men like this became welcome—even if casual conversations, time spent together and loaded smiles did not lead to a romantic relationship, I appreciated the attention and validation of their company. But God had a way of shutting down casual, fruitless encounters. At times, another girl caught the guy's attention. Other times the young man, recognizing my growing interest, politely shut things down and suggested that I deserved better. Only in hindsight did I agree.

That the Christian men I encountered on my college campus, at Christian events or in my circle of friends did not pursue me aroused great anxiety. As I went about my normal activities, I wandered which would bring me in proximity to my future husband. I wandered when someone would offer to take me to the movies or out to dinner. Yes, I was ready for love. You can probably imagine my joy when a godly man did express interest, regularly calling, spending time with me, and taking me to social events. I felt my time had arrived! Even my friends were excited for me.

When the rare prospect came into my life, I prepared to give him my heart. I began imagining what our lives would be like as husband and wife. Because few available godly men came my way, I assumed the one with whom I shared quality time was meant to be my husband. Imagine my disappointment when I learned the feelings weren't mutual. When it became evident that he was neither following through on plans to connect, nor returning my phone calls, I had to accept that this nice Christian man would not be my husband. When he expressed that he enjoyed hanging out with me but didn't wish to pursue a relationship, I had to accept what he said at face value. Rather than trying to manipulate the situation and give him time to realize how loveable I could be, I had to accept that talking to him on the phone or spending time alone with him was unwise. I needed to move on.

Plateau of Comfort
Rarely did men express an interest in me during my relationship journey. Because men rarely asked me out, I jumped at an opportunity to grab a meal with a gentleman. I welcomed the opportunity to spend time talking on the phone with a Christian man. Because I gave in to the myth that it was abnormal to be alone, my Plateau of Comfort remained the place where a male gave me attention. After all, the attention distracted me from the fact that I was "alone." For this reason, I eventually gave my phone number to guys whose advances I'd otherwise never give into—not horrible men, but men with whom I had no intention of pursuing a relationship. Although they raised red flags and caused my friends to worry, these men had access to my time and heart.

Eventually, because of discerning family and friends who wanted the best for me, I had to face the red flags. Any comfort experienced during these short-lived encounters brought no lasting satisfaction. Going through the motions of a relationship could not replace my desire for a deep, meaningful relationship with someone who truly deserved my affection. I chose not to linger in The Plateau of Comfort. I trusted that God had something better. As one friend put it, God would provide me a tailor-made husband.

Valley of One
Inevitably, I ended up in The Valley of One far longer than I anticipated. I did not understand how most of my friends and associates were able to move from one relationship to the next while I awaited my first. I often cried and questioned why no one wanted me. How was it that guys affirmed that I'd be a good

catch yet none ever asked me out? Fortunately, I never questioned my values. Nevertheless, I did question my self-image. I wondered what I lacked that prevented men from pursuing a relationship. I wondered why men preferred other women in my various circles, yet overlooked me.

It must be true that God gives strength to the weary. Despite countless journal entries lamenting my relationship status, God enabled me to live a productive, fulfilling life. The moments I longed to enjoy romantic rendezvous were spent instead nurturing relationships and enjoying the company of friends I cherish to this day. We laughed together, prayed together, danced together, dined together and enjoyed life together.

When I longed to spend quality time with a significant other, I ended up communing with God instead. Often moments of sorrow produced tears that led to prayer and ultimately scripture consultations. As scripture provided insight, comfort, and direction for my life, I wanted to share what I learned with others. Increasingly, God provided these opportunities on my college campus, in my local church, on the job and in my social life. Eager to see others learn and apply scripture to their lives, I pursued opportunities to pour into teens. I started small group fellowships with friends where we studied scripture together, encouraged one another and enjoyed good meals.

The practices and habits that characterize my Valley of One experience God undoubtedly used to prepare me for my present vocation and ministry work. Moreover, as I became increasingly active in the local church and beyond, I realized I could not marry a "pew warmer." For me, a mere church attender would not be a suitable life partner.

Bearing fruit in The Valley of One required pruning. God

had to prune me of various myths that made me long for male companionship. As I observed family and friends showered with gifts from their significant others, I assumed I'd acquire certain things only if I had a man. One of my most liberating moments was when I realized that if I wanted a diamond tennis bracelet, I could buy it myself. I treated myself to meals at my favorite restaurants. Although I desired company, my meal tasted as scrumptious then as the meals I now enjoy with my husband.

Furthermore, God blessed me with generous parents who gave me gifts that significant others often give. One year, after I commented that my mother and sister received the same line of cosmetic goods from the men in their lives for Christmas, my father saw to it that I received the same products on another special occasion. Although these things were material, God showed me that I truly lacked neither essentials nor luxuries just because I didn't have a boyfriend.

God even lifted my spirits on Valentine's Day. While in college, I unexpectedly received a Valentine greeting from a friend. He was kind enough to send these to all of his female friends, "just because." Mindful of how this gesture lifted my spirits, I also use Valentine's Day to remind friends that they are special and loved despite their relationship status. These experiences helped me to cherish and appreciate relationships with God, family and friends, rather than romance. I'm sure my husband will agree that I appreciate all of his romantic gestures—but I value his friendship most.

Furthermore, God needed to purge me of the myth that because men didn't pursue me, I was unattractive. While it took my heart a while to catch up with my head, I came to realize I lacked nothing essential to finding a mate. Rather, my relationship status was the product of God's sovereignty. My sister often told me that God's angels were guarding me. God sought to protect me from relationships that would produce relational baggage and heartache. Although difficult to see at the time, the sorrow of being "alone" was preferable to that produced by bad relationships. The one serious relationship that I'd eventually have proved to be the only one that mattered – my relationship with Jumaine Jones.

Wilderness of Spectating
Before meeting my husband, it seems I had one foot in The Valley of One and the other in The Wilderness of Spectating. While I hoped to earn both my bachelor's degree and "Mrs." during undergrad, I ended up celebrating other family and friends' nuptials and growing families. I stepped into yet another season unattached. As I departed Lexington, Virginia and returned to the DC metropolitan area, I had hopes that my relationship plight would improve.

But despite having more opportunities to meet new people and interact with others, my relationship status did not change. My evenings and weekends were just as lonely as those spent in my college dorm. What's more, as my college career came to an end, all of my siblings were now in relationships. As the eldest child this was a difficult pill to swallow. Can you imagine taking your younger brother to the mall to buy a gift for his high school crush or to deliver a cake he baked for his girlfriend? It was also overwhelming to see most of my friends exploring new relationships and nurturing existing relationships. It seemed I was the only one who couldn't get a date. Late one year my mother said to me, "You know how you get around the holidays. Start praying now." Her unexpected motherly advice was both humorous and what I needed to hear. Fortunately, I obeyed.

In addition to praying for strength, my time as a spectator required that I rejoice and mourn with others. This involved having a listening ear as friends shared relationship woes or responding in joy as friends announced their engagements. As friends gave glory to God for bringing that special someone into their life, I wondered why God continued to overlook me. I wondered how I differed from my peers. But making comparisons led to nothing good. Comparisons only enhanced my sorrow and caused me to think of ways I could change my situation. I turned every corner hoping to meet my husband.

While some may agree that weddings provide a great opportunity to meet a potential companion, these weren't my thoughts when I was invited to attend a friend's wedding in 2002. Excitement about my upcoming travel was soon overshadowed by the fact that I'd miss out on local events that would likely put me in proximity with Christian men I wouldn't otherwise meet. However, I made my way to Georgia and enjoyed spending time with friends and helping the bride prepare for the ceremony. Although single with no prospects, I experienced a Quadrant 4 moment. I was truly happy for my friend and excited for the opportunity to be a part of her special day. I counted it an honor to not only attend the wedding but to help with last-minute details.

I later learned that this weekend in 2002 was the same weekend Jumaine first shared the relationship insights he gleaned from Deuteronomy 2. He shared this message during the event that my travels prevented me from attending. That Jumaine and I met a week later is a testament to God's timing and sovereignty. As a spectator, the temptation to manipulate situations and prioritize opportunities to meet a potential mate is great. I thank God that he allowed me to prioritize my existing relationships that weekend. After all, God showed that when He was ready for me to meet my mate, he would orchestrate events to that end. As a matter of fact, the evening of my friend's wedding, God was at work in Maryland aligning events so I would meet Jumaine in the bowling alley six days later.

Land of Love
Shortly after meeting Jumaine, I recognized him as the type of man I'd like to marry. Not only was he attractive and fun to be around, but he also exhibited fruit of a relationship with Christ. That he was a pastor did not excite me; it was his lifestyle beyond the church doors, his passion for God's Word and a desire to share the gospel with others that impressed me most. That Jumaine was a gentleman, enjoyed music, knew how to sing, possessed fashion savvy, interacted well with my siblings and friends, and went above and beyond to make me happy were added bonuses.

Although excited to marry Jumaine, I didn't fully grasp the extent to which he was my tailor-made husband until after we wed. God knew the type of husband I needed to minister to me and encourage me amidst the challenges and disappointments of life. When I vowed to love, honor and cherish my husband for better or for worse, for richer or for poorer, in sickness and health, the specific hardships and disappointments awaiting us did not enter my mind. Jumaine and I have encountered challenges that tear some marriages apart. Nevertheless, prayer and our individual commitment to God spill over into our commitment to one another. I'm grateful for a husband who loves me despite my imperfections. I'm grateful for a husband willing to prioritize our home and fight for our marriage. The resolve required to move beyond The Mountain of Acceptance and Plateau of Comfort, and to successfully navigate The Valley of One and Wilderness of Spectating, is necessary to persist in The Land of Love.

As God enabled me to persevere during previous phases of my relationship journey, I now depend on Him to help me honor my husband and stay the course in my marriage. Despite the hurdles my husband and I face, I am filled with appreciation and unconditional love for my husband. Jumaine Jones was well worth the wait. The relationship fantasies I conjured as a youth and young adult pale in comparison to the plan God uniquely designed for me.

CONCLUSION

The decisions we make determine the destiny we live. Our lives are shaped by our decisions and we can underestimate the impact of one choice on our entire lives. Although God can turn even our mistakes around for His good, we can never undo a decision.

Throughout the journey, you will be tempted to make unwise decisions. You will be tempted to give in to what feels right in the moment. You will be tempted to ignore the wisdom of those who have gone before you. You will be tempted to rebel against God. You will feel the urge to reject scripture and follow the leadings of your heart, which is prone to deception. You may find yourself captivated by people who are not the healthiest for you. The pressure of trials and conflicts may make you want to run into the arms of someone who is forbidden. The key to experiencing all God has for you from this book is having the courage to make tough decisions. You will have to walk away from good relationships to trust God for what is best, deal with closed doors when you want them to remain opened, and face broken relationships without having a sense of closure on this side of glory. As hard as you may try, you won't be able to fix what is broken and you must avoid entering into romantic relationships to fill a void only God can fill.

You may have completed reading this book, but your journey is still ahead of you. Remember to use this book as a map. You may get lost. You'll struggle to make sense of what seems incomprehensible. Let this book serve as a guide so you know what you need to do to get where God wants you to be. You will also meet others on a similar journey. Share your insights and wisdom with them. Together, we can prevent each other from being lost in love.

CPSIA information can be obtained at www.ICGtesting.com
Printed in the USA
BVOW07s2045260913

332252BV00002B/13/P